INTRODUCING
ISSUES WITH
OPPOSING
VIEWPOINTS®

Self-Injury

Mary E. Williams, *Book Editor*

GREENHAVEN PRESS
A part of Gale, Cengage Learning

GALE
CENGAGE Learning·

Detroit • New York • San Francisco • New Haven, Conn • Waterville, Maine • London

Elizabeth Des Chenes, *Director, Publishing Solutions*

© 2013 Greenhaven Press, a part of Gale, Cengage Learning

For more information, contact:
Greenhaven Press
27500 Drake Rd.
Farmington Hills, MI 48331-3535
Or you can visit our Internet site at gale.cengage.com

For product information and technology assistance, contact us at

Gale Customer Support, 1-800-877-4253
For permission to use material from this text or product, submit all requests online at
www.cengage.com/permissions

Further permissions questions can be e-mailed to permissionrequest@cengage.com

Articles in Greenhaven Press anthologies are often edited for length to meet page requirements. In addition, original titles of these works are changed to clearly present the main thesis and to explicitly indicate the author's opinion. Every effort is made to ensure that Greenhaven Press accurately reflects the original intent of the authors. Every effort has been made to trace the owners of copyrighted material.

Cover image © Jens Stolt/Shutterstock.com.

LIBRARY OF CONGRESS CATALOGING-IN-PUBLICATION DATA	

Self-injury / Mary E. Williams, book editor.
     pages cm. -- (Introducing issues with opposing viewpoints)
 Audience: 14-18.
 Audience: Grade 9 to 12.
 Includes bibliographical references and index.
 ISBN 978-0-7377-6280-8 (hardcover)
 1. Self-mutilation in adolescence--Juvenile literature. 2. Self-injurious behavior--Juvenile literature. 3. Cutting (Self-mutilation)--Juvenile literature. I. Williams, Mary E., 1960- editor of compilation.
 RJ506.S44S448 2013
 616.85'8200835--dc23

2012044473

Printed in the United States of America
1 2 3 4 5 6 7 17 16 15 14 13

Contents

Foreword

Indulging in a wide spectrum of ideas, beliefs, and perspectives is a critical cornerstone of democracy. After all, it is often debates over differences of opinion, such as whether to legalize abortion, how to treat prisoners, or when to enact the death penalty, that shape our society and drive it forward. Such diversity of thought is frequently regarded as the hallmark of a healthy and civilized culture. As the Reverend Clifford Schutjer of the First Congregational Church in Mansfield, Ohio, declared in a 2001 sermon, "Surrounding oneself with only like-minded people, restricting what we listen to or read only to what we find agreeable is irresponsible. Refusing to entertain doubts once we make up our minds is a subtle but deadly form of arrogance." With this advice in mind, Introducing Issues with Opposing Viewpoints books aim to open readers' minds to the critically divergent views that comprise our world's most important debates.

Introducing Issues with Opposing Viewpoints simplifies for students the enormous and often overwhelming mass of material now available via print and electronic media. Collected in every volume is an array of opinions that captures the essence of a particular controversy or topic. Introducing Issues with Opposing Viewpoints books embody the spirit of nineteenth-century journalist Charles A. Dana's axiom: "Fight for your opinions, but do not believe that they contain the whole truth, or the only truth." Absorbing such contrasting opinions teaches students to analyze the strength of an argument and compare it to its opposition. From this process readers can inform and strengthen their own opinions, or be exposed to new information that will change their minds. Introducing Issues with Opposing Viewpoints is a mosaic of different voices. The authors are statesmen, pundits, academics, journalists, corporations, and ordinary people who have felt compelled to share their experiences and ideas in a public forum. Their words have been collected from newspapers, journals, books, speeches, interviews, and the Internet, the fastest growing body of opinionated material in the world.

Introducing Issues with Opposing Viewpoints shares many of the well-known features of its critically acclaimed parent series, Opposing Viewpoints. The articles are presented in a pro/con format, allowing readers to absorb divergent perspectives side by side. Active reading questions preface each viewpoint, requiring the student to approach the material thoughtfully and carefully. Useful charts, graphs, and cartoons supplement each article. A thorough introduction provides readers with crucial background on an issue. An annotated bibliography points the reader toward articles, books, and websites that contain additional information on the topic. An appendix of organizations to contact contains a wide variety of charities, nonprofit organizations, political groups, and private enterprises that each hold a position on the issue at hand. Finally, a comprehensive index allows readers to locate content quickly and efficiently.

Introducing Issues with Opposing Viewpoints is also significantly different from Opposing Viewpoints. As the series title implies, its presentation will help introduce students to the concept of opposing viewpoints and learn to use this material to aid in critical writing and debate. The series' four-color, accessible format makes the books attractive and inviting to readers of all levels. In addition, each viewpoint has been carefully edited to maximize a reader's understanding of the content. Short but thorough viewpoints capture the essence of an argument. A substantial, thought-provoking essay question placed at the end of each viewpoint asks the student to further investigate the issues raised in the viewpoint, compare and contrast two authors' arguments, or consider how one might go about forming an opinion on the topic at hand. Each viewpoint contains sidebars that include at-a-glance information and handy statistics. A Facts About section located in the back of the book further supplies students with relevant facts and figures.

Following in the tradition of the Opposing Viewpoints series, Greenhaven Press continues to provide readers with invaluable exposure to the controversial issues that shape our world. As John Stuart Mill once wrote: "The only way in which a human being can make some approach to knowing the whole of a subject is by hearing what can be said about it by persons of every variety of opinion and studying all modes in which it can be looked at by every character of mind. No wise man ever acquired his wisdom in any mode but this." It is to this principle that Introducing Issues with Opposing Viewpoints books are dedicated.

Introduction

"At the time, I absolutely didn't want anybody to know [I was cutting]. I wanted people to think I had it together, not think I was crazy. Looking back though, I wish someone had been able to see how bad I was hurting inside, and talked to me about it."

—Interviewee, Cornell Research Program
on Self-Injurious Behavior

Singer, songwriter, and actress Demi Lovato started her career at age seven, playing a role on the children's show *Barney and Friends*. At age fourteen, she began appearing in several television comedies; by age sixteen, she was a star in several Disney Channel movies and series. But underneath her growing popularity and outward success, Lovato was deeply troubled. In the seventh grade, a group of girls bullied her, calling her fat and ugly. She became obsessed with losing weight and turned to dieting and bulimia as she struggled to become acceptable and perfect. At age fifteen, she began cutting her wrists and forearms.

Lovato admits that the media played a role in her first experiences with self-injury: "I saw it only on TV, and I wondered what it would feel like."[1] Soon, however, it became a way for her to relieve stress and anxiety. She says, "There were times I felt so anxious, almost like I was crawling out of my skin, that if I didn't do something physical to match the way I felt inside, I would explode. I cut myself to take my mind off that."[2] When fans and gossip columnists began noticing her scars, Lovato's publicists created a cover story, claiming that silicone bracelets were causing the injuries. The attention only increased her anxiety. As Lovato explains, "When someone sees it, it's terrifying, so I started doing it in areas where no one can see."[3]

Referred to variously as self-inflicted violence (SIV), nonsuicidal self-injury (NSSI), or self-mutilation, self-injury describes the actions of those who intentionally hurt themselves in a way that causes tissue damage to the body. It includes a range of behaviors that are not socially accepted and that are usually without suicidal intent, including cutting, scratching, or carving of the skin; burning, slapping, or punching one's body; picking at scabs until they bleed; hitting oneself with a heavy object; pulling out hair; biting oneself; breaking bones; and swallowing toxins. Cutting, burning, and head-banging are the most common forms of self-injury among youths.

What causes people to intentionally harm themselves? Self-injurers themselves report a variety of reasons for this behavior, but most would agree that it is rooted in emotional turmoil. Some self-injurers experience so much inner torment that they find physical pain to be a relief. When emotions are too overwhelming, pain can serve as a kind of release valve during a crisis. During physical injury, the brain releases endorphins, chemicals that relieve pain and that can even induce a euphoric high—making self-harm potentially addictive. Other self-injurers may be in a numbed state, and they hurt themselves to feel *something*, even if the feeling is painful. Although self-injury is not necessarily a symptom of a mental disorder, it is sometimes seen in those who have depression, bipolar disorder, post-traumatic stress disorder, or borderline personality disorder. With these kinds of disturbances, people often cope by suppressing their emotions, eventually shutting down their ability to feel anything. Self-injury then provides a way to "kick-start" sensation. The physical pain becomes preferable to the feeling of emptiness or unreality.

Self-injury is an unhealthy way to cope with confusing or overwhelming feelings, and those who repeatedly harm themselves need counseling and support to confront their problems. However, for self-injurers, the thought of seeking help can become yet another emotional quandary. Young self-injurers especially worry about what others would think if their behavior were discovered. They either fear that they will not be understood or taken seriously—or that their problem will be seen as so disturbing that they will be labeled as mentally ill or dangerous to others. Thus, as was the case with Lovato, many self-harmers go to great lengths to keep their behavior a secret.

Those who suspect that a friend or loved one is self-injuring are also in a difficult situation. They may worry that expressing their concerns to their friend intrudes on their privacy or that their friend will respond with anger or defensiveness. Experts maintain, however, that a friend's self-injury should never be ignored. The genuine concern of another person is often the key to getting a self-injurer to accept the help that they need. According to studies compiled by the Cornell Research Program on Self-Injurious Behavior (CRPSIB), "Individuals who self-injure wish that someone *would* raise the subject—even though it is uncomfortable."[4]

The CRPSIB offers several suggestions for people who suspect that a friend or loved one is self-injuring. First of all, one should approach the self-injurer in private, not in social situations where there are distractions or where others might hear the discussion. During the private meeting, a nonjudgmental and nonalarmist approach is best, and concerns should be raised clearly and gently. The concerned party should show "respectful curiosity," as the CRPSIB explains: "[Invite] your friend to speak freely about his or her experiences. You can do this by asking questions such as 'how does injuring help you feel better?', 'are there things that really trigger you to injure?' Not only does this allow your friend to talk about his or her relationship with self-injury while you fully listen, it can help you understand what he/she is going through and about the role self-injury plays in your friend's life."[5] Self-injurers should be encouraged to talk with a parent, teacher, counselor, or other trusted adult—and they might appreciate a friend's offer to join them to get help. In addition, affirming and commending a self-harmer for any step they take toward getting help provides positive reinforcement. Finally, one should continue engaging in normal activities with a self-injuring friend—so that he or she understands that the friendship continues in spite of personal difficulties. Lovato affirms the importance of supportive relationships: "I surround myself with people who make positive decisions. . . . My friends and I look out for each other, and I just love inviting everyone over to watch TV."[6]

It is in secrecy that painful wounds thrive, experts note. But once self-injurers share their burden with others and learn healthier coping strategies, they eventually stop wounding themselves. *Introducing Issues with Opposing Viewpoints: Self-Injury* explores causes of and solutions to this often-misunderstood issue, providing perspectives that foster concern and compassion for those who hurt themselves.

Notes

1. Quoted in Marjorie Ingall, "Cutting Close," *Tablet Magazine*, May 17, 2011.
2. Quoted in Danielle Paquette, "Demi Lovato Talks Cutting, Eating Disorders in New Interview," *Los Angeles Times*, July 17, 2012.
3. Quoted in Ingall, "Cutting Close."
4. Jackie Goodman and Janis Whitlock, *How Can I Help a Friend Who Self-Injures?* (Pamphlet). Ithaca, NY: Cornell Research Program on Self-Injurious Behavior in Adolescents and Young Adults.
5. Goodman and Whitlock, *How Can I Help a Friend Who Self-Injures?*
6. Quoted in Paquette, "Demi Lovato Talks Cutting, Eating Disorders in New Interview."

Chapter 1

Who Is Affected by Self-Injury?

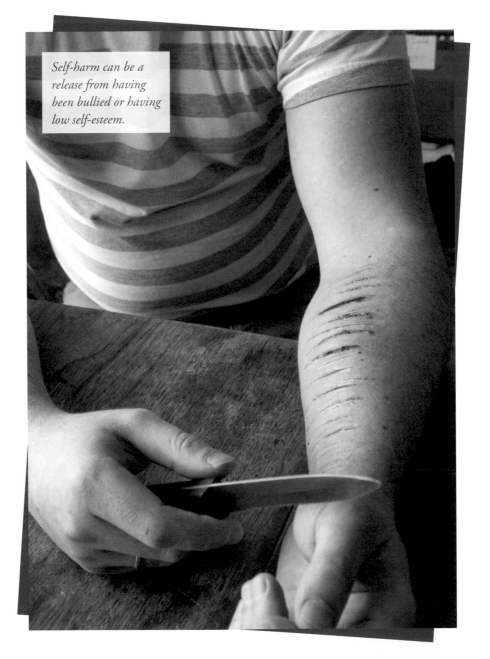

Self-harm can be a release from having been bullied or having low self-esteem.

Self-Harm Figures Soar in a Generation Under Pressure

"'Only a fraction' of cases of self-harm are seen in hospitals, so the true scale of the crisis will be much larger."

Independent on Sunday

Hospitals in England report a striking increase in young people being admitted due to self-injury, notes the *Independent on Sunday* in the following viewpoint. Over the past decade the number of hospitalizations has increased by more than 30 percent among youths under age twenty-five. Since only a small number of self-harm victims end up in hospitals, the extent of the problem is much greater than these statistics suggest, claims the British Department of Health. Self-injury in young people indicates that they are experiencing great emotional distress and are unable to cope with it. With hopes of reducing mental health problems among its population, the British government has launched new strategies aimed at earlier interventions for youths who injure themselves or exhibit other psychological problems. The *Independent on Sunday* is a newspaper in London, England.

AS YOU READ, CONSIDER THE FOLLOWING QUESTIONS:
  1. According to the author, how many British children under age ten were hospitalized for self-injury between 2001 and 2011?
  2. According to officials cited in the viewpoint, what kinds of events trigger episodes of self-harm?
  3. Between 2001 and 2011 which population had the sharpest rise in hospitalization due to self-injury, according to the author?

More than 1,800 children aged under 10 have been hospitalised for self-harming in the past decade, sparking fears of a generation unable to cope with the pressures of childhood.

Last year alone almost 150 boys and girls aged 10 or under were admitted to hospital for intentional self-harm, including more than 80 pre-school children.

The number of girls admitted to hospitals in Great Britain for self-inflicted injuries has risen 44 percent in the last ten years to more than twenty-six thousand cases.

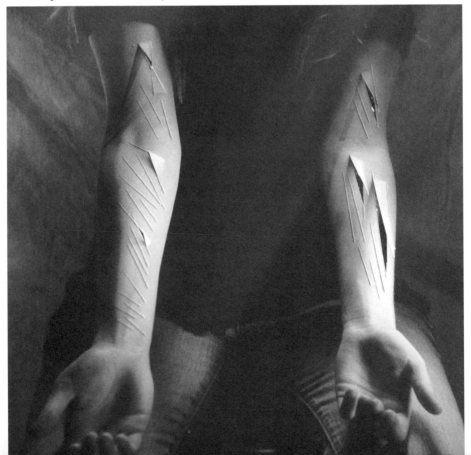

In a sign of a worsening problem, the number of girls and women aged under 25 admitted in the past 10 years has soared by 44 per cent to more than 26,270 in 2010–11. Among boys and men of the same age, the figure has leapt by a third to 11,656. The figures are for hospitals in England.

The Department of Health (DoH) admits that "only a fraction" of cases of self-harm are seen in hospitals, so the true scale of the crisis will be much larger.

"These shocking statistics should act as a wake-up call to everyone who cares about the welfare of young people," said Lucia Russell, the director of campaigns, policy and participation at YoungMinds, a charity which is working with the Government to redesign mental-health services for children. "Self-harm is often dismissed as merely attention-seeking behaviour, but it's a sign that young people are feeling terrible internal pain and are not coping."

> **FAST FACT**
>
> The *Journal of Clinical Psychology* reports that up to 4 percent of the US population—about 12 million Americans—show signs of self-harming behavior.

According to officials, an episode of self-harm is often triggered by an argument or another upset, but can also be linked to bullying, low self-esteem, and worries about sexual orientation.

The Government has promised [pounds sterling] 32m to improve access to psychological therapies for children and young people over the next four years.

Paul Burstow, a Liberal Democrat health minister, told the *Independent on Sunday* that, for too long, mental illness among children was overlooked by the NHS. "It has really suffered from being the poor cousin of mental health, which was itself the Cinderella service. It was not a priority for the NHS.

"For half of all mental health problems in this country the symptoms first show during adolescence. Let's look at the early signs and support families with proper therapies. It is about moving to intervene early."

More than one in 10 children aged 15 to 16 report having self-harmed in their lifetime. However, the DoH insists it is "rare for very young children" to self harm. A million children will have a diagnos-

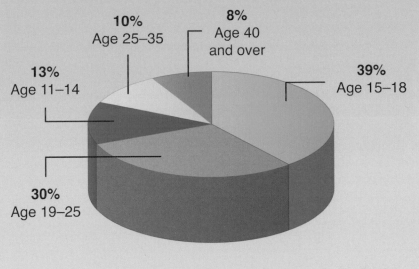

Average Age of Self-Injurers

- 10% Age 25–35
- 8% Age 40 and over
- 13% Age 11–14
- 39% Age 15–18
- 30% Age 19–25

able mental-health disorder. Childhood mental illness costs up to £59,000 per child every year.

The rise in hospital admissions has been steepest among women aged 17 to 25, rising by 50 per cent between 2001 and 2011.

Separate figures released last week show 40,000 under-25s were rushed to A&E in 2009–10 after self-harming, up from 36,000 in 2007–08.

Earlier this year, the Government launched a new strategy, No Health Without Mental Health, to tackle the problem. Officials are working with young people, parents and YoungMinds to redesign specialist services for children, focussing initially on cognitive behavioural therapy and parenting therapy.

Ministers hope to reduce by as much as 40 per cent the number of people in adulthood who have mental health problems. The economic and social costs of mental health in the UK are almost [pounds sterling] 100bn.

Last month a study by the charity Mind warned that a combination of rising demand and spending cuts was threatening the viability of mental health services.

EVALUATING THE AUTHOR'S ARGUMENTS:

The *Independent on Sunday* reports that self-harm can be connected to bullying, low self-esteem, and concerns about one's sexual orientation. In response, the British government has pledged to offer young people more access to psychological counseling in the years to come. Do you think that early intervention and therapy will decrease the amount of self-injury in Great Britain? Why or why not?

Self-Injury Has Increased Among Soldiers

Tony Dokoupil

"There are some soldiers who will do almost anything not to go back [into combat]."

Self-harm is a rising trend among US soldiers serving in Iraq and Afghanistan, reports Tony Dokoupil in the following article. The stress of long, repeated combat tours drives some troops to try to avoid returning to war by intentionally wounding themselves. While soldiers have been known to resort to self-injury in previous wars, the problem seems to be compounded in these more recent conflicts, the author points out. Dokoupil is a senior writer at *Newsweek* magazine.

AS YOU READ, CONSIDER THE FOLLOWING QUESTIONS:

1. In what ways have soldiers recently inflicted injuries on themselves, according to the author?
2. According to Dokoupil, about how many US soldiers were discharged for self-harm between 2003 and 2008?
3. In the author's view, why may the wars in Iraq and Afghanistan lead to more instances of self-harm than previous wars have?

A s an internist at New York's Mount Sinai Hospital, Dr. Stephanie Santos is used to finding odd things in people's stomachs. So last spring [2007] when a young man, identifying himself as an Iraq-bound soldier, said he had accidentally swallowed a pen at the bus station, she believed him. That is, until she found a second pen. It read 1-800-GREYHOUND. Last summer, according to published reports, a 20-year-old Bronx soldier paid a hit man $500 to shoot him in the knee on the day he was scheduled to return to Iraq. The year before that, a 24-year-old specialist from Washington state escaped a second tour of duty, according to his sister, by strapping on a backpack full of tools and leaping off the roof of his house, injuring his spine.

A Rising Trend

Such cases of self-harm are a "rising trend" that military doctors are watching closely, says Col. Kathy Platoni, an Army Reserve psychologist who has worked with veterans of Iraq and Afghanistan. "There

During a Pentagon news conference, Colonel Elspeth Ritchie, a doctor in the Office of the Army Surgeon General, discusses efforts to study and understand suicides among American soldiers in Iraq and Afghanistan.

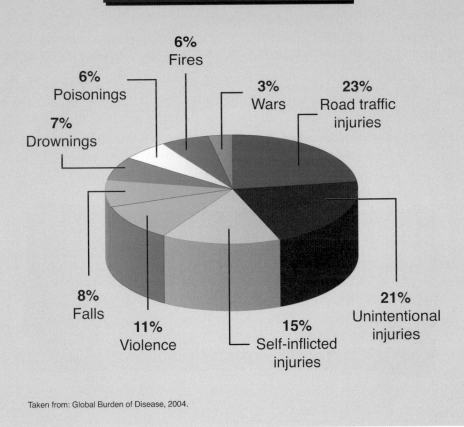

Causes of Injury Deaths

- 6% Fires
- 6% Poisonings
- 7% Drownings
- 3% Wars
- 23% Road traffic injuries
- 8% Falls
- 11% Violence
- 15% Self-inflicted injuries
- 21% Unintentional injuries

Taken from: Global Burden of Disease, 2004.

are some soldiers who will do almost anything not to go back," she says. Col. Elspeth Ritchie, the Army's top psychologist, agrees that we could see an uptick in intentional injuries as more U.S. soldiers serve long, repeated combat tours, "but we just don't have good, hard data on it." Intentional-injury cases are hard to identify, and even harder to prosecute. Fewer than 21 soldiers have been punitively discharged for self-harm since 2003, according to the military. What's worrying, however, is that American troops committed suicide at the highest rate on record in 2007—and the factors behind self-injury are similar: combat stress and strained relationships. "It's often the families that don't want soldiers to return to war," says Ritchie.

Soldiers have long used self-harm as a rip cord to avoid war. During World War I, the *American Journal of Psychiatry* reported "epidemics of self-inflicted injuries," hospital wards filled with men shot in a single finger or toe, as well as cases of pulled-out teeth, punctured eardrums and slashed Achilles' heels. Few doubt that the Korean and Vietnam wars were any different. But the current war—fought with an overtaxed volunteer Army—may be the worst. "We're definitely concerned," says Ritchie. "We hope they'll talk to us rather than self-harm."

EVALUATING THE AUTHOR'S ARGUMENTS:

Tony Dokoupil notes that a few soldiers have been prosecuted and discharged for intentionally harming themselves. Do you believe that self-injury should be a punishable offense for people in the armed forces? Why or why not?

YouTube Videos of Self-Injury Are an Alarming Trend

"[Self-injury] is being depicted in hundreds of YouTube clips—most of which don't carry any warnings about the content."

Roni Caryn Rabin

Many experts are disturbed by the popularity of YouTube videos depicting self-injury, reports Roni Caryn Rabin in the following viewpoint. These videos are often graphic, mixing music and words with images of people cutting, burning, hitting, or biting themselves. The danger of these videos is that they can lead youths to believe that self-injury is normal or even glamorous, the author points out. In addition, images of self-injury can "trigger" people who have a history of the behavior—that is, it can heighten their urge to harm themselves. Few of these videos contain clear messages about seeking help for self-injurious behavior, Rabin notes. Rabin is a health reporter for the *New York Times*.

YouTube videos are spreading word of a self-destructive behavior already disturbingly common among many teenagers and young adults—'cutting' and other forms of self-injury that stop short of suicide, a new study reports.

As many as one in five young men and women are believed to have engaged at least once in what psychologists call nonsuicidal self-injury. Now the behavior is being depicted in hundreds of YouTube clips—most of which don't carry any warnings about the content—that show explicit videos and photographs of people injuring themselves, usually by cutting. They also depict burning, hitting and biting oneself, picking at one's skin; disturbing wounds and embedding objects under the skin. Most of the injuries are inflicted on the wrists and arms and, less commonly, on the legs, torso or other parts of the body.

FAST FACT

Triggers for self-injury can include emotional tension, a painful experience, or images of blood and self-harming activities.

Disturbingly Popular Videos

Some of the videos weave text, music and photography together, which may glamorize self-harming behaviors even more, the paper's authors warn.

And the videos are popular. Many viewers rated the videos positively, selecting them as favorites more than 12,000 times, according to the new study, in the March [2011] issue of the journal *Pediatrics,* whose authors reviewed the 100 most-viewed videos on self-harm.

Stephen P. Lewis, assistant professor of psychology at the University of Guelph in Ontario and the paper's lead author, calls the YouTube depictions of self-harm "an alarming new trend," especially considering how popular Internet use is among the population that engages most in self-injury already: teenagers and young adults.

"The risk is that these videos normalize self-injury, and foster a virtual community for some people in which self-injury is accepted, and the message of getting help is not necessarily conveyed," Dr. Lewis said. "There's another risk, which is the phenomenon of 'triggering,' when someone who has a history of self-injury then watches a video or sees a picture, his or her urge to self-injure might actually increase in the moment."

Mixed Messages

Only about one in four of the 100 most-viewed videos sent a clear message against self-injury, the paper's analysis showed, and about the same proportion had an encouraging message that suggested the behavior could be overcome. About half the videos had a sad,

Number of Online Self-Injury Message Boards Established by Year

Year	Number of Boards	Total Membership
1998	1	93
1999	7	949
2000	26	2,831
2001	25	703
2002	28	1,611
2003	19	952
2004	24	806
2005	38	1,698
Total	168	9,643

Taken from: Janis L. Whitlock et al. "The Virtual Cutting Edge: The Internet and Adolescent Self–Injury." *Developmental Psychology*, vol. 42, no. 3, 2006.

melancholic tone, while about half described the behavior in a straightforward and factual manner.

About a quarter of the videos conveyed a mixed message about self-injury, while 42 percent were deemed neutral and 7 percent were clearly favorable toward self-injury.

Only 42 percent of the videos warned viewers about the content.

EVALUATING THE AUTHOR'S ARGUMENTS:

The experts that Roni Caryn Rabin quotes in her viewpoint maintain that YouTube videos depicting self-injury often weave images and music together and thus "glamorize" self-harming behavior. Considering what you know on this topic, do you agree that such videos make self-injury seem acceptable or attractive? Explain your answer.

Self-Injury Among Youths with Eating Disorders Is an Alarming Trend

Dianne Klein

"Researchers found that 40.8 percent of patients with eating disorders ... had documented incidents of intentionally harming themselves."

In the following viewpoint Dianne Klein discusses research from Stanford University and the Lucile Packard Children's Hospital that reveals that almost half of the hospital's patients with eating disorders also engage in self-harming behavior. However, many health-care providers do not ask their anorexic and bulimic patients if they injure themselves, so the numbers of self-injurers in that population may be higher than this study reports, according to Klein. Moreover, the fact that patients are not usually screened for self-harm suggests that the current profile of the self-injurer (an older white female with a history of substance abuse) is flawed, the author notes. Klein writes for *Inside Stanford Medicine*, an online magazine produced by the Stanford University School of Medicine in Stanford, California.

AS YOU READ, CONSIDER THE FOLLOWING QUESTIONS:
1. How did the researchers conduct their study about self-injury among patients with eating disorders, according to Klein?
2. What was the average age of patients who were identified as self-injurers, according to the author?
3. In the opinion of physician Rebecka Peebles, as cited by the author, why do people injure themselves?

An alarming number of adolescents already battling eating disorders are also intentionally cutting themselves, and health-care providers may be failing to diagnose many instances of such self-injury, according to a new study from Stanford University School of Medicine and Lucile Packard Children's Hospital.

The researchers found that 40.8 percent of patients with eating disorders in their study had documented incidents of intentionally harming themselves, most often by cutting and burning. What's more, the study suggests that inadequate clinical screening might mean the count should be much higher.

"These are very high numbers, but they're still conservative estimates," said the study's lead author, Rebecka Peebles, MD, who was an instructor in pediatrics at Stanford when the research was conducted and is joining the faculty at Children's Hospital of Philadelphia.

More Screening Is Needed

Peebles noted that clinicians aren't routinely asking about this activity. "We ask 97 percent of children 12 years and up if they smoke cigarettes; we need to get that good with screening for self-injurious behavior," she said.

The study was published online Oct. 8 [2010] in the *Journal of Adolescent Health*. Its senior author is James Lock, MD, PhD, professor of psychiatry and behavioral sciences and of pediatrics. He is also psychiatric director of the Comprehensive Eating Disorders Program at Packard Children's Hospital.

To conduct the study, the researchers examined the intake evaluation records of 1,432 patients, ages 10–21, who were admitted to the hospital's eating disorders program from January 1997 through April 2008. Just over 90 percent of all the patients were female, three-quarters of them white, with a mean age of 15. Among the 40.8 percent identified to be physically harming themselves, the mean age was 16. Many of these patients had a history of binging and purging, and 85.2 percent of the self-injurers were cutting themselves.

The researchers also discovered that slightly fewer than half the charts showed that health-care providers had asked patients if they intentionally injured themselves. If patients aren't asked, they are unlikely to volunteer such information, said Peebles.

Those who were questioned tended to fit previously published profiles of a self-injurer: older, white, female, suffering from bulimia nervosa, or with a history of substance abuse. "The question is, 'Are we missing other kids who are not meeting this profile?'" Peebles said. "This is part of why we wanted to look at this. If you see an innocent-looking 12-year-old boy, you don't even think of asking about self-injurious behavior. We need to get much better about universal screening."

Peebles noted that the profile itself might be flawed. If health-care workers only ask a certain type of patient about a behavior, the profile that emerges will necessarily reflect that bias, she said.

FAST FACT

According to the website Eating Disorder Help, self-injurers are often perfectionists who dislike their bodies. The same is true for people with eating disorders.

"Trying to Feel Pain"

The study did not examine the reasons behind such acts but Peebles said her clinical experience suggested patients "are trying to feel pain."

"Patients describe a feeling of release that comes when they cut or burn themselves," she said. "They'll cut with a razor or a scissor blade. Sometimes we've even had kids who will take the tip of a paperclip and gouge holes. To burn themselves, they'll heat up a metal object and press it to their skin, or they'll use cigarettes."

Physicians and other health-care providers at Packard's Comprehensive Eating Disorders Program now question all new

Growing numbers of adolescents with eating disorders are also intentionally cutting themselves, according to a study from Stanford University.

patients about self-injurious behavior. Studies have shown that between 13 and 40 percent of all adolescents engage in some form of self-injury, which is also associated with a higher risk of suicide.

"In clinical practice, kids are fairly open when you engage with them," Peebles said. "They'll come in wearing long sleeves, or hiding the marks on their inner thighs. But then when you ask them, they are usually willing to discuss the behavior."

The study's other author is Jenny Wilson, MD, who was a resident in pediatrics when the study was conducted.

EVALUATING THE AUTHOR'S ARGUMENTS:

As Dianne Klein explains, experts have underestimated the prevalence of self-injury among youths with eating disorders. How does the study she cites highlight the problem of assumptions and bias in research? Explain.

Study Looks at Self-Harm in Young People

European Union News

> *"[Researchers] point out that self-harm is one of the strongest predictors of suicide."*

The following viewpoint from *European Union News* is a summary of a study on self-harm conducted by researchers in Great Britain and Australia and originally published in the journal *Lancet*. Conducted over a period of several years, the study found that 8 percent of teens deliberately injure themselves and that depression, anxiety, antisocial behavior, and substance abuse are frequent symptoms among youths who self-harm. While only a fraction of those surveyed report having suicidal intentions, the researchers note that self-injury is a strong predictor of suicide. This is probably because self-harmers often have mental-health issues that go untreated, which increases their risk for suicide. The author concludes that anyone who engages in self-harm needs immediate attention and should seek counseling and medical advice.

"One in 12 people self-harm in their teenage years," the BBC has reported. For most people the problem will resolve before adulthood, but for 10% it will continue into their adult lives, it continued.

This alarming statistic, estimated in an Australian study, corroborates existing estimates that around 8% of UK teens deliberately harm themselves.

This well-conducted new research surveyed almost 2,000 Australian adolescents over a period of several years, assessing them from around 14–15 years of age until they were into their late 20s. It found that between the ages of 14 and 19, 8% of the sample, mainly girls, reported they had self-harmed. Self-harm in adolescence was significantly associated with symptoms of depression and anxiety, antisocial behaviour, high-risk alcohol use, and smoking cannabis and tobacco.

A substantial drop in reported self-harm occurred as adolescents grew into young adults, though adolescent depression and anxiety were linked to self-harm in young adulthood.

There are some inherent problems that come with researching areas such as self-harm, particularly in making sure that the information provided by participants is accurate and that the numbers who self-harm are not underestimated. Also, it should also be noted that though the researchers found associations between self-harm and various psychosocial factors in adolescence, the study's design cannot demonstrate the specific causes why.

Though this carefully conducted study suggests that although most adolescent self-harm may resolve spontaneously, this does not undermine the importance of the issue, and that it can be a sign of greater mental health problems that may eventually lead to continuing self-harm or even suicide. Self-harm can take many forms and may be associated with various emotional, personal or lifestyle circumstances.

Any individual that self-harms requires immediate and supportive care and attention, and should seek medical help or advice immediately.

Where Did the Story Come From?

The study was carried out by researchers from King's College London, and the Murdoch Children's Research Institute, the University of Melbourne and Deakin University in Australia. It was funded by the National Health and Medical Research Council of Australia and by the Government of Victoria.

The study was published in the peer-reviewed medical journal the *Lancet*. It was reported at length by *BBC News* and the *Guardian*, with both including comments from external experts.

What Kind of Research Was This?

This was a cohort study that looked at patterns of self-harm from middle adolescence to early adulthood, in a sample of 1,943 adolescents. This type of study, which enables researchers to follow up large populations over lengthy periods, is often used to examine health outcomes and how they relate to lifestyle factors. However, when factors are assessed at the same time (e.g. self-harm and other lifestyle factors in adolescence) it can only demonstrate associations, and cannot show that any one factor directly caused a particular outcome.

FAST FACT

About 33 percent of people who have suicidal thoughts eventually attempt suicide, reports Harvard University psychologist Matthew Nock.

The researchers define self-harm as an act with a non-fatal outcome in which an individual deliberately initiates behaviour (such as self-cutting) with the intention of harming themselves. They point out that self-harm is one of the strongest predictors of suicide and is par-

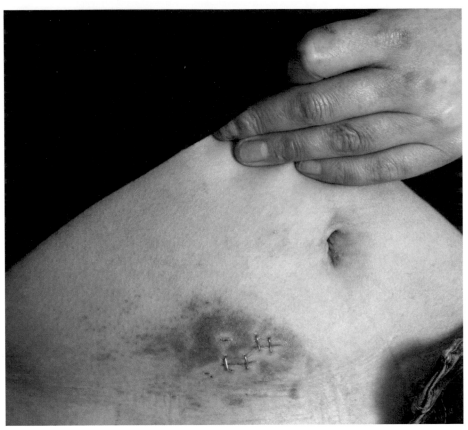

This knife wound and bruise were self-inflicted. Studies show that approximately 8–10 percent of teens self-harm, and a smaller percentage attempt suicide.

ticularly common in 15- to 24-year-old women, among whom rates are thought to be rising. However, little is known about the natural history of self-harm, especially during the transition from adolescence to early adulthood. Charting the course of self-harm during this period might help provide insight into the risk factors for future suicide, they say.

What Did the Research Involve?

Between 1992 and 1993, the researchers recruited a random sample of 2,032 schoolchildren aged 14–15 from 45 schools in Victoria, Australia. The schools were chosen at random and included government-run, Catholic and independent schools, with numbers reflecting the proportion of children this age in different types of schools.

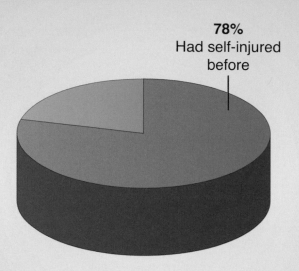

78%
Had self-injured
before

Taken from: Moya L. Alfonso. *The Tip of the Blade: Self-Injury Among Early Adolescents.* University of South Florida graduate dissertation, 2007.

Participants were asked to fill in questionnaires and give interviews by telephone both at the start of the study and in various "waves" of follow-up, generally conducted when the participants were aged between 16 and 29. Waves one and two were formed of two different classes with separate entry points to the study. Waves three to six took place at six-monthly intervals, from 14 to 19 years, with three follow-up waves in young adulthood, aged 20–21 years, 24–25 years and 28–29 years. Based on the time and way that these various waves were assessed, the researchers grouped responses into several waves for their analysis.

In waves one to six, participants answered questionnaires on laptop computers, with telephone follow-up of those absent from school. In young adulthood, only computer-assisted telephone interviews were used.

Out of the 2,032 students initially recruited, 1,943 participated at least once during the first six waves. One school dropped out after wave one.

The adolescent participants were asked about self-harm from wave three to nine. They were asked whether they had deliberately hurt themselves or done anything they knew might have harmed or even killed them during a recent period (one year during wave three, and six months for the other waves). Those who said they had self-harmed were then asked for more detailed information, including on suicide attempts.

The researchers also asked the adolescents in waves three to six about their use of cannabis, tobacco, high-risk alcohol intake (calculated according to national guidelines), symptoms of depression and anxiety, antisocial behaviour and parental separation or divorce. Where relevant, their responses were assessed and categorised using standardised interview questions and symptom scales.

The researchers used standard statistical methods to identify patterns of self-harm and any association between self-harm and other factors. . . .

What Were the Basic Results?

Overall, 1,802 (88.7%) of the participants responded in the adolescent phase. The main findings were as follows:

- 8% of adolescents (149 individuals, 10% of girls and 6% of boys) reported that they had self-harmed
- More girls (95 out of 947, 10%) than boys (54 out of 855, 6%) reported self-harm (risk ratio 1.6, 95% confidence interval (CI) 1.2 to 2.2)
- The self-harm reported was most often burning or cutting behaviour
- Less than 1% of adolescents reported having suicidal intentions
- There was a reduction in the frequency of self-harm during late adolescence, with the decline continuing into young adulthood
- In the young adult phase, the proportion of all participants reporting self-harm fell to 2.6% (46 of 1,750 interviewed between ages 20 and 29)
- Of those who had completed assessments both in adolescence and young adulthood (1,652), 7% (122) had self-harmed in adolescence but now no longer did so in adulthood, and only 0.8% (14) had self-harmed both in adolescence and adulthood. Some 1.6% (27) had started self-harming for the first time in adulthood

- During adolescence, self-harm was independently associated with symptoms of depression and anxiety (hazard ratio 3.7, 95% CI 2.4 to 5.9), antisocial behaviour (1.9, 1.1 to 3.4), high-risk alcohol use (2.1, 1.2 to 3.7), cannabis use (2.4, 1.4 to 4.4), and cigarette smoking (1.8, 1.0 to 3.1). Direct causation between these factors cannot be demonstrated
- Adolescent symptoms of depression and anxiety were significantly associated with self-harm in young adulthood (5.9, 2.2 to 16).

How Did the Researchers Interpret the Results?

The researchers conclude that most self-harming behaviour in adolescence 'resolves spontaneously', i.e. tails off without any formal intervention. However, they point out, young people who self-harm often have mental health problems that may go untreated. Treating anxiety and depression in adolescence could be an important strategy in preventing suicide in young adults, they add.

Conclusion

This carefully conducted study focuses on the important issue of self-harm during adolescence and its association with mental health problems such as depression and anxiety. Even if, as this study suggests, most adolescent self-harm may naturally resolve itself, untreated mental health problems may contribute to an increased risk of continuing self-harm or even suicide.

It should be noted that the study was conducted in Australia, where patterns of self-harm may be different from those in the UK. That said, the figure agrees with the estimates from UK organisations such as the National Institute for Health and Clinical Excellence, which calculates that around one in 12 15–16 year olds self-harms. The Mental Health Foundation places the figure at between one in 12 and one in 15 young people.

Also, the study relied on participants to reliably and truthfully report episodes of self-harm. Relying on participants to self-report these behaviours introduces the possibility of error, and these findings could even be an underestimate of the true prevalence; this could particularly apply to the results when young adults had their assessment interviewed by telephone, which might make it harder to openly discuss any self-harm. Checking against hospital records could possibly give a more accurate estimate, although as the authors rightly point out, most individuals who self-harm do not present to medical care.

Although the study had high response rates, the estimates generated from the overall responses could also be subject to further inaccuracy as only 51% of participants completed every "wave" of assessments.

It should also be noted that though the researchers found associations between self-harm and various psychosocial factors in adolescence, direct causation cannot be demonstrated between self-harm and any one factor due to the cross-sectional nature of this assessment. In short, while we have found that self-harmers were more likely to act or feel certain ways, such as being depressed, the design of this study means we cannot assume that we have identified a particular factor or cause behind the association.

Self-harm can take many forms and may be associated with various emotional, personal or lifestyle circumstances. Any such individual requires immediate and supportive care and attention, and should seek medical help or advice immediately.

For more information please visit: http://www.nhs.uk/.

EVALUATING THE AUTHOR'S ARGUMENTS:

What evidence does the *European Union News* use to support the argument that self-injury is a strong predictor of suicide? Do you think that this data backs up the author's assertion? Why or why not?

Self-Injury Is Usually Non-Suicidal

Raychelle Cassada Lohmann

"Generally people who self-harm do not wish to kill themselves; whereas suicide is a way of ending life."

In the following viewpoint Raychelle Cassada Lohmann describes the differences between self-harm and suicide. The most important difference is intent, she says. Those attempting suicide intend to end their lives, while self-harmers do not intend to end their lives, although they may accidentally inflict lethal harm on themselves. Suicide is an escape from the pain of life, while self-harm is a means of coping with the pain of life, the author contends. In addition, self-harm can release chemicals that produce euphoria and so make the self-harmer feel good for a short time. Lohmann is a National Board–certified counselor, who has worked in middle school and high school settings and is the author of *The Anger Workbook for Teens*.

AS YOU READ, CONSIDER THE FOLLOWING QUESTIONS:

1. What are seven common means of doing self-harm, according to the author?
2. As stated in the viewpoint, what are the five main reasons for doing self-harm?
3. What are the six main reasons Lohmann cites that people give for committing suicide?

Hayden's Story:

Hayden sat at his desk hands shaking. Tears splattered onto his papers and ink ran off of the pages. Why wouldn't they stop? "fag, worthless, good for nothing, stupid, sissy, ugly, dumbo." Why do they hate him so much? Why did he hate himself so much? He was a disgrace, worthless, an utter disappointment. These thoughts and more raced throughout his mind. Reaching into his desk drawer he pulled out his faithful pair of scissors and pulled back the neck of his shirt. Scarred pink welts told the story of past cuts. With the blades of the sharp scissors he began to dig and carve into his flesh; creating a fresh wound on his youthful skin.

Colton's Story:

Colton sat on the edge of his bed hands shaking. He looked in his closet where a noose swung from the ceiling. The time had arrived. This is what he'd been planning for a while. He had tried everything and nothing worked. There was only one way to take care of it . . . to end it. Numbness set into his body and a wave of nausea swept through him. "It's time" he thought. He stood and made his last descent. Each step was one step closer to ending the pain. . . .

How similar are the two scenarios? How different are they? Both clearly have troubled individuals, who are hurting. But in regards to the ending result, both scenarios are very different. One scenario describes self-harm while the other involves the taking of one's life.

Self-harm is thought to be directly linked with suicide but this isn't the case. The two are actually as different as night and day. Unfortunately the two oftentimes get grouped together because both are inflictions of pain and sometimes people who begin with self-harm may later commit suicide. Generally people who self-harm do not wish to kill themselves; whereas suicide is a way of ending life.

One significant difference between suicide and self-harm is intent. Simply put, a suicidal person sees no other way out and wants to end his or her life. People who are contemplating suicide are experiencing life stressors and possibly depression in which they don't have an escape. Suicide is their attempt to escape pain and suffering, and not burdening loved ones any longer. Suicidal acts usually come from a place of hopelessness, depression and worthlessness. The underlying mindset between someone who is suicidal and someone who self-harms is very different.

On the flip side, many people who self-harm view hurting themselves as a way of coping with life. In fact, for some, the self-infliction of pain reassures them they are still alive. This is especially true when they are experiencing emotional numbness or feeling disconnected with the world around them. Plus, self-harming can cause changes in the brain chemistry, which gives the effects of a "rush" and can easily become addictive and highly dangerous.

Clear differences between the two:
Self-harm is a form of mutilation while suicide is the deliberate taking of one's life.

What is self-harm?
Self-harm is the intentional and deliberate hurting of oneself. Most commonly it is done by:

- Cutting
- Burning
- Hitting
- Picking at the skin
- Pulling hair
- Biting
- Carving

What are the warning signs of self-harm?

- Many cuts/burns on the wrists, arms, legs, back, hips, or stomach
- Wearing baggy or loose clothes (e.g., wearing hoodies or long sleeves during hot days to conceal the wounds)
- Always making excuses for having cuts, marks or wounds on the body
- Finding razors, scissors, lighters or knives in strange places (i.e., the nightstand drawer or under the bed)
- Spending long periods locked in a bedroom or bathroom
- Isolation and avoiding social situations

Why do people self-harm?

- To escape their feelings
- To cope with life stressors

- To express their pain
- To punish themselves (Some people mutilate their bodies to punish themselves for what's going on in their lives. They lack the appropriate coping skills and suffer from low self-esteem so they feel that they deserve what they are doing to themselves.)
- To feel euphoria. (It's true. When we get hurt endorphins are released into the blood stream, resulting in a "natural high" or a feeling of euphoria. Self-harming behaviors can be addictive and habit forming.)

What is suicide?
Suicide is the voluntary and intentional act of taking of one's life. Suicide is commonly carried out through:

- Firearms (number one method by men and women)
- Hanging (most commonly done by men)
- Drug Overdose (most commonly done by women)

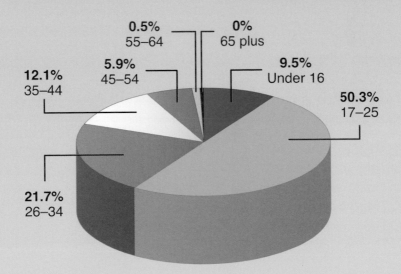

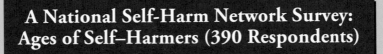

Taken from: National Self-Harm Network, 2009.

Men are four times more likely to die from suicide than women, but women attempt suicide more often during their lifetime. http://www.medicinenet.com/script/main/art.asp?articlekey=84760

The warning signs of suicide:
While some suicides may occur without any warning signs, most people who are suicidal do give warnings, such as:

- Increasing their alcohol and/or other drug use
- Taking unnecessary risks and impulsivity
- Threatening suicide and/or expressing a strong wish to die
- Exhibiting rage and/or anger
- Talking about wanting to die or to kill oneself
- Fascinating over or preoccupying oneself with death
- Talking about feeling hopeless or having no reason to live
- Talking about being a burden to others
- Acting anxious or agitated; behaving recklessly
- Isolating or withdrawing oneself
- Displaying mood swings
- Telling loved ones goodbye
- Setting one's affairs in order
- Giving things away, such as prized possessions
- Referring to death via poetry, writings and drawings
- Exhibiting dramatic changes in personality or appearance
- Changing eating or sleeping patterns
- Declining in performance

Why do people commit suicide?
Fellow PT [*Psychology Today*] blogger Alex Lickerman provides a detailed explanation in his blog "The Six Reasons People Attempt Suicide: Suicide is far more understandable than people think."
Here are the top six reasons:

1. They're depressed
2. They're psychotic
3. They're impulsive
4. They're crying out for help
5. They have a philosophical desire to die
6. They've made a mistake

The difference between the mindset of a self-harmer and a person contemplating suicide:

There's a difference in the mindset of a self-harmer and someone who is suicidal. The major difference is that of "intent". With suicide the intent is to bring end to one's life; to end pain and suffering. Conversely, with self-harm the intent is one of trying to find relief and release from emotional pain and distress.

Most people who engage in self-harming do so as a means to cope with their distress (avoid suicide) rather than escape it by committing suicide. Self-harm is a response to painful emotions. Unfortunately self-harm may become a habitual way of coping with stress.

The injuries caused by self-harm may be serious or superficial, but any form of self-mutilation is a sign of emotional distress and should be taken seriously. Self-harm is oftentimes confused with suicidal behavior. A person who self-harms does not intend to commit suicide, but their self-injurious behavior may result in an accidental death.

EVALUATING THE AUTHOR'S ARGUMENTS:

Raychelle Cassada Lohmann, the author of this viewpoint, maintains that most self-injurers do not have suicidal intentions. The author of the previous viewpoint, *European Union News,* on the other hand, contends that self-harm is a "strong predictor of suicide." In your view, is one of these viewpoints more accurate than the other? Or do both viewpoints make equally valid points? Explain your answer.

Chapter 2

Why Do People Injure Themselves?

Teens deliberately injure themselves for a variety of reasons.

Viewpoint

1

Only Skin Deep

Chloe, as told to Sandy Fertman Ryan

"My self-esteem was so low that whenever I was totally upset, I'd pull out the scissors."

In the following viewpoint Chloe, a seventeen-year-old girl, recounts her personal history of self-injury to author Sandy Fertman Ryan. As a young teen Chloe never felt comfortable talking about her problems with other people. When she became overwhelmed with school pressures and family conflicts, she began cutting her arms, ankles, and hips with scissors. The painful sensations became a kind of release for her—a way to cope with feelings of anxiety, frustration, and depression. Chloe eventually found effective therapy with a counselor and joined a peer support group at her school.

AS YOU READ, CONSIDER THE FOLLOWING QUESTIONS:
1. What grade was Chloe in when she began cutting herself, as stated in the viewpoint?
2. According to Chloe, how did Chloe's best friend find out that she was injuring herself?
3. What does Chloe do to help other teens who are facing emotional difficulties, according to the viewpoint?

Sandy Fertman Ryan, "Only Skin Deep," *Girls' Life*, vol. 14, no. 4, February/March 2008, p. 76. Copyright ©

*I*magine if you weren't allowed to talk about your feelings. Ever. You could gossip, joke, discuss mundane things, like school assignments, but no feelings allowed! You'd probably explode, right? That's exactly how Chloe felt . . . before she began cutting herself.

All kids get stressed, but many get to talk it out. For me, that didn't seem like an option. My relationship with my parents wasn't good, and although I had a lot of friends and a brother and sister, I've never felt comfortable telling anyone my problems. I hated the thought of people feeling bad for me or thinking I was a complainer. And my parents didn't like to hear it, so I pretty much put on a happy face. That's probably why I started cutting myself.

In seventh grade, when I was 13, I had my first boyfriend—whom I'm still seeing. At the time, my parents forbade me to go out with him, partly because I was too young but also because they didn't like him. That was the beginning of a downhill slide in my relationship with them. Since I was not going to stop seeing my boyfriend, I lied to them all the time, and whenever I was caught—which was often—I got grounded. I tried so many times to talk things out with my parents, but they just would not listen, so I basically shut down, I'd come home from school and go to my room and hide out.

My parents surely mean well but they were extremely controlling, making all my decisions for me. They also pressured me about grades, friends and basically everything I did. They wanted me to be perfect. It seemed they definitely expected more of me than they did of my siblings. They thought I didn't push myself enough. I'd look at my friends who were close with their parents and wish I had what they had.

The Last Straw, the First Cut

In eighth grade, everything imploded. I was overwhelmed with school and my parents, so without thinking I went into my kitchen, got the scissors out of a drawer, and cut myself on my wrist. The weird thing is, I wasn't scared. I didn't even consider that I could have killed myself. It bled and stung, but for some odd reason, it felt good. I pushed on the cuts to continue feeling the sting. I felt a sense of release . . . and calm. Strange, but it felt good to punish myself.

I knew it was horrible, but I couldn't stop. From then on, I always used the scissors to cut myself. I never showed anyone my cuts, because I was ashamed, but my boyfriend noticed and asked me what had happened. For the first time, I lied to him and said I'd scraped myself. I felt terrible about being dishonest with him. He was worried, though, so he went to my best friend and told her about it. She was so upset that she nagged me until I finally admitted I had been cutting myself. She told me I had to stop, but once again, I lied, promising never to do it again.

My cuts were on my arms, so I could hide them, and on my ankles, so they would look like sports injuries. I also started cutting my hips since nobody but me ever saw them. I was clumsy anyway, so it was easy for others to believe I'd had an accident. Still, I felt really embarrassed. Because I knew the truth.

Hurts So Good

There was no pattern or regularity to my cutting, but my self-esteem was so low that whenever I was totally upset, I'd pull out the scissors. My cuts were never life-threatening, so I never had to go to the hospital. I'd try to control myself, but that was extremely difficult. The cutting had actually become addictive.

If people were to look at me, they'd never imagine I was a girl who would intentionally hurt herself. But I did. Knowing that made me feel worse—so I'd cut myself more! I felt I wasn't strong enough to handle things most other people could; I hated myself for that.

Oddly enough, other [than] the self-mutilation, my life was normal. I got great grades, I played soccer and field hockey, and I had a lot of friends. It was like I had two lives. Around my friends, I always acted like I was happy. But when I was by myself, I felt extremely lonely and angry, like an outsider looking in. And even though I was cutting myself in my own house, my parents had no idea what was going on.

I kind of resented the fact that my friends and family didn't just magically know about my problem and offer to help me. That was so unfair of me to expect, though, because I never let anyone get that close to me.

Whenever I felt the need to cut myself, I felt frustrated, angry, stressed, depressed, confused and anxious all at once, and that was too much for me to handle alone. Cutting myself was my only sense of control over my life since I had absolutely none at home.

Self-harm can be an emotional release for some youth—a way to cope with anxiety, frustration, and depression.

Truth or Consequences

When I was a sophomore, my boyfriend had had enough. He was the only one who knew I was still doing it, and he said, "You have to stop. If you don't, I can't be with you." He hated seeing me hurt myself and threatened to tell someone if I didn't get help immediately.

I was devastated. I knew I couldn't take it anymore. I decided to see a therapist. I didn't tell my parents about my cutting, but they were very supportive about getting me counseling. I didn't tell her about my cutting right away, but it came up pretty quickly. She focused on the fact that I always kept everything inside and helped me understand the impact of letting those feelings build up.

I finally told my mom. We were having a huge fight, and I blurted, "I used to cut myself, and it was all your fault!" My mom cried, but she really didn't say anything. I'd hoped it would somehow make her realize how hard they had been on me, but that didn't happen.

Even though my problems with my parents haven't been resolved, I know cutting is not the answer. Therapy is now my release. I have a place where I can express myself and be heard.

I've had one relapse. It was in 11th grade, and I was having a really bad day. I'd done poorly on a test and was scared of how my parents would react. It sent me over the edge. I cut my arm deeply, and that scar is my worst. Afterward, I felt terrible about what I'd done, so I promised myself I'd never do it again—and I haven't for over a year now.

Her "Life Support"

I still see my therapist, which makes all the difference. I also have a peer support group at school. We meet weekly to talk about everything that stresses us.

I also volunteer at Teen Line (1-800-852-8336), a helpline where I answer phones and talk to kids about their problems—which actually helps me with mine, too. I know that one day I will get a call from a teen who self-harms, and I'll have so much to offer. What I've gone through has taught me to be more understanding of other people's problems. I used to think, "What kind of weirdo cuts herself?" But now I know it's not about cutting or anorexia or doing drugs—it's about emotional problems that need to be dealt with.

When I look at the scars on my body, it doesn't make me sad. It really makes me aware of all I've been through—and how far I've come.

Sadly, teen self-abuse is increasing at an alarming rate. Studies reveal 15 to 20 percent of teens have intentionally hurt themselves—and more of those are girls. Often, these teens have experienced trauma, such as the death of a parent or abuse. But even some without traumatic events in their lives become self-injurers. What do most have in common? Ninety percent report that they have families who discourage emotional expression. Not long ago, teens who hurt themselves were considered mentally ill, but it's now considered a way (although unhealthy) of coping with stress. Self-harm is usually done by cutting, burning, scratching, biting, pinching or hitting. Which begs the question. Why do so many girls torture themselves? Experts say a common reason is to gain a perceived sense of control when life seems chaotic. The physical pain is bearable to some teens, while emotional pain is not. Some, however, do it for the opposite reason. They feel so numb from earlier trauma that they actually want to feel something. Others hurt themselves as a form of self-punishment for feelings of inadequacy and worthlessness. Surprisingly, most self-injurers are not suicidal. In fact, it is often a way of avoiding suicide. Still, why such extreme measures to handle stress? Kids are often pressured to do too much—get good grades, play sports, participate in after-school activities and so on. Add to that the fact that parents are overworked and stressed themselves, so teens often shy away from burdening them with their problems. As a result, teens may lack a good support system—which can spell disaster. If you or someone you know is hurting herself (or even considering it), please, talk about your feelings to someone you trust, whether a teacher, counselor, coach or parent.

Need Help?

If you have the desire to cut yourself, understand that it can be fatal. Write in a diary, or even on your arms. If you're cutting, it's time to get help. These places offer information and resources for self-injurers.

1-800-DONTCUT This hotline is sponsored by S.A.F.E. (Self Abuse Finally Ends) Alternatives and offers a list of therapists around the country who help self-injurers.

youngwomenhealth.org/si.html The site provides info about why girls cut themselves, constructive alternatives to cutting, books about self-injury and info about what to do if a friend is cutting herself.

psyke.org Get real stories from teens who cut, recommendations for other cutting websites and blogs, and poetry from self-injurers.

> **EVALUATING THE AUTHOR'S ARGUMENTS:**
>
> Both Chloe's boyfriend and her best friend were upset when they discovered that she was cutting herself. How would you react if you found out that a close friend was injuring herself or himself? Considering what you have read elsewhere in this volume, what do you think would be the most helpful thing you could do for a friend who self-harms?

Viewpoint 2

A Cry for Help

Hara Estroff Marano

"It's imperative to stop self-mutilation as soon as it's discovered, as cutting can take on a life of its own with addiction-like qualities."

The degree of emotional relief that self-injury provides can become addictive, explains the author in the following selection. Self-injury is not a suicidal attempt to end life but an impulsive act to control mood. Self-harmers do so to distract themselves from intense emotional pain, so, although the act is not suicidal, it should be treated as a serious symptom. The release from emotional pain and tension lasts only a few hours, so a safer and more long-term solution is needed. Hara Estroff Marano is an author, journalist, and editor at large of *Psychology Today* for the past fifteen years, although not a trained psychologist.

AS YOU READ, CONSIDER THE FOLLOWING QUESTIONS:
1. What percentage of counseling center directors report an increase in cases of self-injury, according to the author?
2. Who is Armando Favazza and what does he say self-injury is the opposite of, as stated in the viewpoint?
3. What does Favazza say about the issue of control?

*I*ncidents of self-harm continue to grow among young women. Though not necessarily a prelude to suicide, it is indicative of depression or anxiety.

Sudden epidemic or gradual increase over the years? Either way, self-mutilation is a huge and growing problem that "has now reached critical mass and grabs our attention," says Russ Federman, Ph.D., director of counseling and psychological services at the University of Virginia.

Nearly 70 percent of counseling center directors report increases in cases of self-injury such as deliberate cutting or cigarette burning of body tissue. "It's now on all our radar screens," Federman notes. "It gets talked about with deans."

Self-harm is not a diagnostic category, so its exact incidence is unknown. But women are twice as likely to do it as men. And it typically accompanies a range of conditions—borderline personality disorder, eating disorders, anxiety and depression. It most commonly occurs, however, in antisocial personality disorder, accounting for a high rate of self-harm in prisons.

FAST FACT

According to self-injury expert Wendy Lader, natural opiates are released during bodily injury. This can increase the addictive potential of self-harm.

It's highly disturbing for a student to walk into her dorm and find her roommate cutting her thighs or arms with shards of glass. Further, self-injury always mobilizes a crisis response; suicidal intent must be ruled out.

Self-harm is a serious symptom, says Federman. "But it isn't about taking one's life. It freaks others out. But rarely does cutting constitute imminent danger to the self. There's not usually suicidal ideation."

Self-mutilation is "the opposite of suicide," insists Armando Favazza, M.D., professor and vice chairman of psychiatry at the University of Missouri, author of *Bodies Under Siege: Self-Mutilation in Psychiatry and Culture* and a leading authority on the subject. "Those who do it want to live. They do it to feel better. It's an impulsive act done to regulate mood."

It is an extremely effective treatment for anxiety, he points out. People who do it report it's "like popping a balloon." There's an immediate release of tension.

It serves "an important defense—distraction," adds Federman. "In the midst of emotional turmoil, physical pain helps people disconnect from intense emotional turmoil." But the effect lasts only hours.

Further, "it is the only action that can effectively stop dissociative episodes," says Favazza. "That makes it especially common among girls who were sexually abused."

Too, self-mutilation has to do with self-punishment. Not to be overlooked is the sense of power it confers. "It allows students to take control of painful processes they feel are out of control, especially chaotic relationships," says Federman.

Sometimes it's a cry for help. Cutting is usually a private process and the scars are hidden. But some people will cut an arm and don a short-sleeve shirt.

Girls have been found to be more susceptible to self-harm because they tend to be more anxious about life than boys are.

Although most cutting is a private act, Favazza reports that he knows of cutting parties—groups of girls who get together to cut in each other's presence. And some students like to hang out with the cutters. That has given rise to "pseudo-cutters," those who cut not to gain release but to belong to a social group.

It's imperative to stop self-mutilation as soon as it's discovered, as cutting can take on a life of its own with addiction-like qualities. Treatment usually involves psychotherapy plus SSRI antidepressants, which decrease the impulsivity behind most acts of self-harm.

EVALUATING THE AUTHOR'S ARGUMENTS:

In this viewpoint author Hara Estroff Marano points to several indicators that suggest that self-injury might be addictive. Review the viewpoints in this chapter and develop a list of such indicators. Do you think that self-harm is addictive? Why or why not?

Media, the Internet, and Nonsuicidal Self-Injury

"[Various] forms of media may serve as vectors for the introduction and contagion of self-injury."

Janis Whitlock, Amanda Purington, and Marina Gershkovich

Evidence suggests that the media have an effect on the rate of self-injury among young people, maintain Janis Whitlock, Amanda Purington, and Marina Gershkovich in the following selection. As part of a research study, the authors tracked the number of songs, movies, and news stories with references to self-injury over a period of several years. They found that there has been a steady increase in the number of self-harm references since the 1990s—and this may be contributing to what many currently believe to be an epidemic of self-injury in the United States. Whitlock, Purington, and Gershkovich are all research scientists with the Cornell Research Program on Self-Injurious Behavior in Adolescents and Young Adults.

Tracy struggles with her emotions, visibly frustrated and angered by the contentious interactions with her mother and her best friend. She lives with her single but warm and attentive mother and brother in a working-class California neighborhood. At 13, Tracy is the epitome of a junior high schooler—worried about fitting in, growing up, and reconciling a somewhat turbulent past with the promise of future independence. One night, after a particularly volatile exchange with her mother followed by a disappointing experience with her best friend, Tracy's agitation is palpable. At the pinnacle of her distress, Tracy makes her way to the bathroom and reaches for a pair of small scissors stored in the vanity. Although a typical part of bathroom paraphernalia, the scissors serve a particular and unusual function for Tracy. Sinking to the floor, she slides the sharp edge across her wrist—lightly enough to avoid serious injury, but deep enough to cause blood to well up as it slowly passes over the delicate skin. On her wrist lie the telltale signs of other, similar moments. After one long cut, she lets the blades fall drunkenly from her hand as she covers her wounds with her shirtsleeve—already stained with dried blood. As Tracy sits crumpled on the floor, the camera zooms out and the scene assumes a slightly fuzzy focus. Sirens wail low and distant in the background. Viewers may or may not realize that the shot is patterned after a typical drug scene in which an addict shoots up and nods off in the middle of an inner-city slum. No viewer, however, will miss the effect of the act—Tracy is now very calm; her anxiety soothed by a "drug" she has not had to buy, steal, or imbibe.

Tracy's story, the central narrative of the film *Thirteen* (Beva, Chasin, Fellner, Hunter, & Hardwick, 2003), is important for many reasons. One of these is that her self-injurious response to stress is reflective of what some have called a new "epidemic" among youth (Brumberg, 2006; Galley, 2003; Welsh, 2004). Although lack of baseline data prohibits empirical validation of this assumption, there is a reasonably high degree of consensus about the likelihood of its validity among youth-focused service providers (N. L. Heath, Toste, & Beettam, 2006; Whitlock, Eells, Cummings, & Purington, in press). The second reason Tracy's story is important is because the public display of her self-injury, available to millions of viewers, has become an increasingly common scene in movies, television shows, and Web-based video media. At least 14 pop icons publicly revealed self-injurious habits from 1993 to 2004 (Beller, 1998; Conroy et al. 1998; Diamond, 1999; C. Heath, 1993, 1998a, 1998b, 2001, 2004; "Holmes reveals," 2005; Maerz, 2001; Ro, 2000; Villa 65,1995; Weiss, 1998; Wurtzel, 1994). Although not all possessed widespread popular appeal, celebrities such as Princess Diana, Johnny Depp, Angelina Jolie, and Christina Ricci all publicly admitted to nonsuicidal self-injury (NSSI) and shared detailed information about how and why it worked for them. Although not intended to promote self-injury, such high-profile disclosures do serve as avenues for dissemination of ideas that in epidemio-

FAST FACT

The 2003 American drama *Thirteen*, about a troubled girl who self-injures, was cowritten by its teenage costar, Nikki Reed. The film is loosely based on Reed's experiences.

logical terms may serve as vectors for contagion. Scenes and themes of self-injurious behaviors have also appeared in popular television shows such as *Seventh Heaven*, *Degrassi*, *House M.D.*, *Grey's Anatomy*, *Nip/Tuck*, and *Will and Grace*. Although Tracy's practice of NSSI is a behavior foreign to most adults, it is anything but novel to most contemporary adolescents—in part because self-injury is now firmly part of the media landscape.

The remainder of this chapter is dedicated to a review of literature, theories, and a nascent empirical study germane to the role of the media on NSSI. We begin with a review of the forms of mass communication available daily to most individuals within and outside of the United States followed by a brief discussion of empirical linkages between media exposure and NSSI, aggression, and suicide. We then present preliminary findings from our study of the links between self-injury and media and examine several of the key theoretical mechanisms through which media and the Internet may influence youth

The 2003 film Thirteen *was based on one young girl's actual experiences with self-injury.*

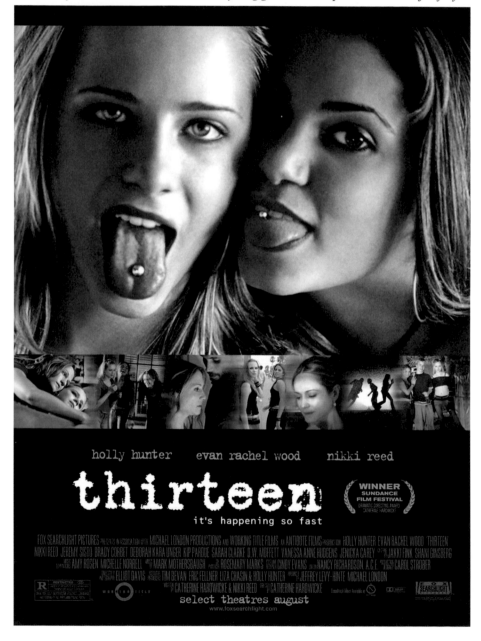

behavior. Finally, we discuss implications for clinical practice and community-based intervention.

Vectors for Communication . . . and Contagion

In 1975, most American families owned or had access to a television, a radio, a phone, and a mailbox. Some received newspapers. By 2006, media routes into and out of the average American home had nearly tripled. Not only had technologies for these basic 1975 media modalities expanded considerably with the advent of cable, satellite, home message recorders, VHS and DVD, and "express" mail deliveries, but wholly novel technologies were developing as well. Personal computers, iPods, handheld camcorders, wireless technology, smart phones, and the Internet are just some of the common fixtures of the contemporary American home media ecology. In the span of less than one generation, opportunities for receiving and sending communications have fundamentally transformed the way individuals connect with information and others outside their proximal environments.

One result of these changes is that today's children and adolescents live media-saturated lives. The sheer multiplicity and pervasiveness of opportunities to both receive and send information has rendered the diffusion of ideas easily accomplished. In a nationally representative study of 8- to 18-year-olds (Roberts, Foehr, & Rideout, 2005), researchers found that 99% of American homes possess at least one television, and 60% of children ages 2 to 18 live in a home with three televisions. More than 70% of children ages 2 to 18 have in-home access to video game consoles, and 86% of youth ages 8 to 18 report at least one computer; 74% live in homes with an Internet connection. On average, a typical U.S. child between 8 and 18 years of age is likely to live in a home equipped with three televisions that probably receive a cable or satellite signal, three VCRs or DVD players, three radios, three CD-tape players, two video game consoles, and a personal computer. In all likelihood, the computer is connected to the Internet and supports instant messaging. Despite the popularity of interactive media, however, older forms of screen media still dominate young people's media exposure. Indeed, more than two thirds (68%) of youth ages 11 to 14 have televisions in their bedrooms, where parental oversight of use is limited. Although the average youth reports spending nearly 6.5 hours per day using media (including the

Internet), he or she is exposed to more than 8.5 hours per day of media messages. Referred to as media multitasking, this seeming paradox arises as a by-product of the fact that for one quarter of the time in which youth use media, they report using two or more simultaneously (Roberts et al., 2005).

In 1979, well before the media revolution, the much revered psychologist Urie Bronfenbrenner articulated what has become foundational work on the ecology of human development (Bronfenbrenner, 1979). In his reckoning, the media was regarded as a distal influence with developmental leverage far secondary to that of the real people and institutions in children's lives—parents, peers, schools, and other important adults and institutions linked to them geographically or through extended family networks. Today, however, peers and even adults who live hundreds or thousands of miles away and without connection to an individual's local family or peer network can assume a pivotal and influential role in a person's life with the mere click of a mouse.

It is not surprising that well-articulated theory and investigation about the full spectrum and magnitude of these changes on human interaction, development, behavior, and life trajectory has not paralleled the rapidity of the media revolution. Most research to date has been conducted on the effects of screen (i.e., what is often thought of as unidirectional) media in which audiovisual systems that deliver content that does not depend on directive responses from the viewer (e.g., television, cinema and movies, music, print news). The Internet, however, provides an array of interactive, or bidirectional, media in which communications functions are built into traditional screen systems (e.g., Internet, telephone, satellite-based telecommunications such as cell phones and smart phones).

Empirical study of the role that bidirectional or interactive media plays in real-life behavior is less than a decade old. Most commonly, these studies target the Internet, broadly conceived. As with unidirectional media, most of the studies do find effects, although these vary greatly in magnitude and nature. In large part this is because bidirectional media forms allow for much more nuanced types of exchange and effect because users may actually be interacting with real individuals through a virtual medium. For example, studies show that Internet use permits the development of positive bonding through formation of social ties which some individuals find difficult to construct offline (Hampton & Wellman, 2003; Kavanaugh & Patterson, 2001). They also suggest, however, that Internet use may increase isolation in real life, expose and reinforce maladaptive self-narratives, or permit the networking of individuals with offline agendas that are dangerous to society (Becker, Mayer, Nagenborg, El-Faddagh, & Schmidt, 2004; Norris, Boydell, Pinhas, & Katzman, 2006; Whitlock, Powers, & Eckenrode, 2006; Ybarra & Mitchell, 2005). Similarly, access to information unavailable locally facilitates information gathering and resources otherwise inaccessible (Borzekowski, Fobil, & Asante, 2006) that can advance educational objectives, and thus academic performance, in children with less reliable access to high-quality education (Jackson et al., 2006). It may also, however, permit vulnerable individuals to readily identify and view potentially damaging content (Ybarra & Mitchell, 2005).

In contrast, unidirectional media is both better researched and easier to understand, in large part because it does not permit exchange or message coconstruction as do the Internet and other bidirectional media modalities. Three decades worth of experience with unidirectional media affirms the potency of influence—especially for adolescents and children (Brown et al., 2006; Escobar-Chaves et al, 2005; Gould, 2001; Huesmann, Moise-Titus, Podolski, & Eron, 2003; Johnson, Cohen, Smailes, Kasen, & Brook, 2002; Paik & Comstock, 1994). For example, every study included in a 2006 special issue of *Archives of Pediatrics & Adolescent Medicine* found significant main effects for media on all child and adolescent behaviors examined. Such findings are not unique. Virtually every media study on the relationship between media and aggression, for example, shows a strong, direct relationship. Indeed, the relationship is so consistently documented that in July 2000, six major professional societies, including the American Psychological Association, the American Medical Association, and the American Academy of Pediatrics, issued a joint statement about its effects. Grounded in a review of more than 1,000 studies, the statement acknowledged as fact the now well-documented empirical link between on-screen violence and child and adolescent behavior and called for coordinated policy responses (Cook et al., 2000).

The mechanisms behind such influence are complex. Although it would be naive to assume that media causes behavior, such as self-injury, research overwhelmingly shows that media plays an important role in disseminating behavioral innovations, in normalizing novel behaviors, and in "priming" through the creation of scripts, which may slowly prepare viewers, particularly young viewers, to try or adopt behaviors they may never have considered. Most scholars attribute the well-documented relationship between media and aggression to the sheer volume of images young media viewers absorb. For example, the 3-year National Television Violence Study (NTVS) analyzing more than 10,000 hours of programming in the United States found that 61% of all programs and nearly 67% of children's programs contained violence. On average, the authors concluded, children view about 10,000 acts of violence per year, a figure that exceeds the amount and severity of violence that actually occurs in the United States (Center for Communication and Social Policy, 1998).

Image prevalence, however, is not the only empirical link to real-life behavior; mere suggestion seems to matter as well. The power of media suggestion was first documented in the 18th century when Goethe penned *The Sorrows of Young Werther*, a novel in which the main character dies by suicide. Following publication of the book in 1774, a rash of suicides prompted several regions to ban it for fear of more (Marsden, 1998). The possible association between media messages and behavior went uninvestigated until Emile Durkheim (1897/1997), well known for his work on suicide, went in pursuit of the answer. His study found no conclusive evidence that social factors, such as imitation, influenced suicide rates. Durkheim's proclamation effectively ended the scholarship in this area until 1974, when another empirical study of the same question documented a link. Phillips's (1974) study reviewed suicides publicized in *The New York Times,* the *New York Daily News,* the *Chicago Tribune,* and the *London Daily Mirror* and showed a clear association between published stories about suicide and subsequent completed suicides in the area in which the story was published. More recent studies found similarly that the magnitude of the increase in suicides and suicide attempts following a suicide story is proportional to the amount, duration, and prominence of media coverage (Gould, Jamieson, & Romer, 2003; Stack, 2000).

How a character or scene is portrayed matters as well. For example, in the vast majority of the programs reviewed as part of the NTVS, violent perpetrators were portrayed as heroes of the stories, and victims rarely suffered pain (Center for Communication and Social Policy, 1998). Similarly, in a review of suicide contagion studies, Stack (2000) found that reports based on newspaper accounts, celebrity suicides, real rather than fictional suicides, and suicide attempts rather than suicide deaths are more likely to inspire copycat effects. Not all groups are at the same risk of media effects. Research consistently shows adolescents and young to be particularly vulnerable to reports and depictions of suicide and aggression in the mass media (Bushman & Huesmann, 2006; Gould et al., 2003).

Empirical Study of Self-Injury and the Media

Because it is likely that many of the same factors critical in linking media and aggression of suicide may be at work with self-injury (with or without suicidal intent), we set out to examine the extent and characterization of self-injury in unidirectional media, bidirectional media, and on the Internet. The study objectives were modest and aimed primarily at documenting the quantity, form, and characterization of self-injury available in contemporary media outlets, with particular attention to Internet message boards and movies, music, and news articles. The Internet message board–focused component of this work found that self-injury Internet message boards are numerous, very easily accessed, and highly frequented; 406 were identified in January 2005, and there were more than 500 a year later. We also found that once online, individuals do much of what they do— namely, seek and provide support and information—offline. They also exchange and share strategies for ceasing the behavior, finding help, avoiding detection, treating severe wounds, and even for injuring in new or different ways (Whitlock et al., 2006). Like the complex story emerging from Internet-focused research, the findings hold hope and caution for those interested in understanding and addressing the role the Internet plays in self-injury (Whitlock et al., 2006; Whitlock, Lader, & Conterio, 2007) and clearly signal the need for additional research in this area.

Our investigation of the role the media plays in disseminating self-injury is less well developed but merits consideration of the findings to date. Although identifying the point at which self-injury began to surface in community populations in more than isolated pockets is impossible, we have endeavored to estimate and track the entry and spread of self-injury images and stories in movies, songs, and print news. We have also conducted content analyses of movies in which self-injury is depicted. The method, results, and interpretation of our findings follow.

Method

Study of the link between self-injury and media is fraught with limitations. The primary limitation is that there exists no standardized mechanism for identifying media forms, such as movies, television shows, and music, in which self-injury appears. The only exception to this limitation is print news, in which search engines such as LexisNexis and Factiva do permit systematic search of current and archived print news by keyword. With these limitations in mind, we began building a database of movies, songs, and print news in which self-injury appears in early 2004. Our first task was to simply document frequency of each by year. The second task, particular to movies, was to code for specific content with attention paid to the way characters were portrayed. What follows is a preliminary summary of our findings to date.

We identified movies and songs featuring self-injury content by sending out regular inquiries to personal and professional networks about whether they had seen a movie with NSSI scenes or knew of songs with NSSI lyrics; through regular visits to NSSI message boards and YouTube sites, where members often discuss music, movies, and television shows with NSSI content; and by visiting two Web sites that include specific references for NSSI media and literature (http://anthol ogy.self-injury.net/section/nonfictional litetatute.php and http://imdb. com). Self-injury news stories were identified in a far more systematic fashion through querying of the LexisNexis search engine using multiple terms including self-injury and self-mutilation. All news articles identified were counted, even if they originated from the same story (such as an Associated Press article) because including all provides a snapshot of the degree of market penetration. Coding of movie content was accomplished through independent viewing, and coding was done by trained student coders. As shown in Table 8.1, movies were coded to capture (a) sex, race, age, and socioeconomic status of the self-injurious characters; (b) self-injury form; (c) presence of comorbid mental illness and degree of suicidal intent; and (d) extent to which self-injurious characters were portrayed as strong (vs. weak) and appealing (e.g., likely to be someone with whom viewers would identify).

Table 8-1. Nonsuicidal Self-Injury (NSSI) Characters

Variables	Self-injurious characters, % (n) (N=43)
NSSI character profile	
Sex	
Male	41.9 (18)
Female	58.1 (25)
Age	
Under 12	2.4 (1)
12–20	28.6 (12)
21–30	31.0 (13)
31–40	23.8 (10)
Over 40	14.0 (6)
Race	
Caucasian	100% (44)
Socioeconomic status	
Low	21.4(9)
Middle	47.6 (20)
High	31.0 (13)
Character appeal	
Strength	
Strong	61.5 (26)
Weak	39.5(17)
Character Appeal	
High	79.5 (34)
Low	20.9 (9)
NSSI form	
Form	
Cutting	61.5 (24)
Bruising	12.8 (5)
Other	15.4 (6)
Burn	7.7 (3)
Stab	2.6 (1)
Comorbidity with mental illness and suicide	
Presence of comorbid mental illness	
Overt (diagnosed)	23.1 (10)
Implied	46.2 (20)
None	30.2 (13)
Suicidality	
Attempt	17.9 (7)
Completion	17.9 (7)
None	67.4 (29)
Intervention	
Mental health treatment	25.6(11)
Physical health treatment	7.7 (3)
Both mental and physical health treatment	5.1 (2)
No formal treatment	61.5 (26)

Character strength and appeal were coded dichotomously. To establish intercoder reliability, coding for all movies was compared across coder dyads. Agreement was assessed by calculating the proportion of codes each individual in the pair coded the same. Intercoder agreement across all pairs was 90%, and discrepancies were discussed until agreement was reached.

Results

As of spring 2007, a total of 47 movies that feature unambiguous NSSI scenes or characters had been identified. Examples included *Thirteen*, *A Lion in Winter*, *Secretary*, *Sid and Nancy*, and *The Scarlet Letter*. Of these, 11 included scenes suggestive of NSSI behavior but not overtly referenced, so they were excluded in these analyses. Of the remaining 36, all but 1 were coded as "drama," 16% (n = 6) "horror," 11% (n = 4) "biography," 11% (n = 4) "action," and 5.5% (n = 2) "romance"; movies could fall into more than one genre category. Most, 72.2% (n = 26), were rated R, 22.2% (n = 8) were rated PG-13, and the remaining 2 were unrated.

Eighty-nine songs with self-injury references had been identified by the same date. Although song genre is difficult to quantify, the vast majority (86.7%) could be classified as some type of rock (e.g., alternative, emotional, gothic, heavy metal, punk), 4.8% as pop, and 6.0% as rap.

Figure 8.1 shows the publication date ranges of both movies and songs over time. The upward trend in both categories is striking. Only 2 movies with unambiguous self-injury references or scenes prior to 1980 were identified. In contrast, between 2000 and 2005, we identified more than 50 songs and 20 movies. Extreme caution in interpreting this trend is warranted because it may be largely due to an artifact of the methodology used to identify data sources. However, self-injury news stories exhibit a similar trend, as shown in Figure 8.2. Because one can systematically search for news stories by keyword, the validity of these data is far more certain.

As shown with movies and music, there exists a clear upward linear trend over time. Evidence of self-injury in print news media prior to 1990 was quite rare—we identified only 253 stories between 1966 and 1990. In contrast, from 2000 to 2005, we identified 1,750 stories alone, with a steady increase each year.

Figure 8-1. Movies and Songs with Self-Injury Referenced by Year

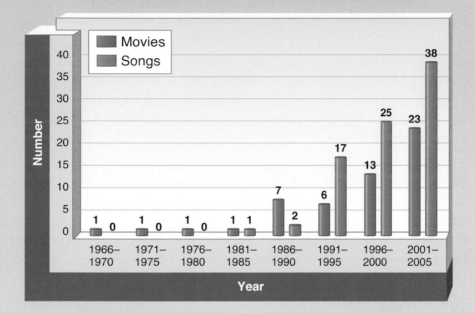

Figure 8-2. Self-Injury-Focused Print News Stories by Year

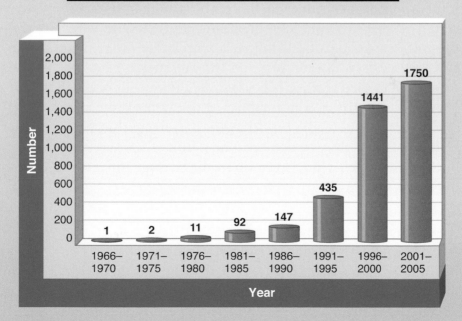

Analysis of movies with self-injury scenes reveals interesting trends across characters. The 36 movies coded featured 43 characters with explicit self-injury experience. As is evident in Table 8.1, the majority, although not by a large margin, were female (58.1%) and in their teens (28.6%), 20s (31%), of 30s (23.8%). Only one was depicted as less than 12 years of age, and the remainder (14%) were portrayed as over 40. All of the self-injurious characters were identified as White, and the majority (78.6%) as of middle to high socioeconomic status. Most (61.5%) were portrayed as strong characters likely to elicit empathy from viewers (79.5%). Most cut (61.5%) and had overt or implied mental illness (69.3%), but only about one third (35.8%) were depicted as having attempted or completed suicide. The majority (61.5%) received no mental or physical treatment for their self-injury during the course of the movie.

In general, the trends observed across time, movie, and character are quite consistent with mainstream perception of the behavior and those who practice it. Considered together, the evidence suggests that media may serve as at least one source of the contemporary public perception of the "self-injurer" as a White female "cutter"—of the 36 movies coded, nearly half (46.6%) included a White female shown cutting; all but 2 of these were featured in movies made since 1995. Furthermore, although definitive evidence about changes in the prevalence of self-injury in media over time will forever be lacking, our data show, with certainty, that it is quite prevalent now. The extent to which increasing media coverage of self-injury, as part of narrative, news stories, and focused conversation (e.g., on Internet message boards), spreads or reinforces the behavior is beyond the purview of research to date. However, in light of well-established research on the effect of uni- and bidirectional media on behavior, it is likely that future studies of this relationship will demonstrate a link. To what, however, can one attribute such a link? How do media leverage influence? To these questions one must turn to theory for answers.

Theoretical Explanations for the Effect of Media and the Internet on Self-Injury

No single theory is sufficient to explain human behavior. Human beings are dynamic; the human mind acts as an associative network in which concepts, emotions, and ideas may become activated by related stimuli in ways impossible to predict or model. For example, viewing a violent scene, whether self- or other-directed, may prime individuals for aggressive thoughts, emotions, and scripts. Such priming and its subsequent effects may occur outside of awareness and through cues only remotely connected to aggression. How does this happen? Sociocultural theories are those designed to explain how the external world affects internal developmental processes. The external social worlds in which individuals grow, through engagement in activities, which require cognitive and communicative functions, promote and shape developmental options and trajectories (Kublin, Wetherby, Crais, & Prizant, 1998; Vygotsky, 1934/1986). A subset of these theories goes far in helping to explain the effect media has on behavior.

Convergence and Emergent Norm Theories

Convergence theory, first described by Turner and Killian (1972), holds that individuals will seek out and converge around a set of mutual interests. Such impulses, for example, are likely to dictate the media content and virtual communities to which individuals become attracted. *Emergent norm theory* adds to this the idea that although individuals in a group will consciously or unconsciously alter their behavior to conform to what they perceive to be group norms, groups are also dynamic in that, once established, they give rise to new and novel norms as they progress (Turner, 1964). The tendency to form groups and to generate new norms may be particularly salient for adolescents and young adults because by middle childhood peers occupy a primary role in development.

Emergent norm theory is most applicable to bidirectional media modalities. The role of the virtual world, such as Internet message boards, blogs, or YouTube, in permitting self-injury groups to form around a shared behavior is an example of these theories and, in particular, of the way they work in tandem. In these contexts, individuals converge around a set of shared behaviors out of which new norms may arise. For example, virtual communities are formed through convergence, through shared interest in self-injury. Once founded, through small acts of support, censure, and sharing, members establish a set of expectations to guide exchange. Depictions of self-injury posted by members may become attractive or normalized to others over time simply because of the perceived commonalities shared by the group. These online experiences may subsequently shape offline expectations and, ultimately, behavior. Similar processes may be at work in unidirectional media as well, where the "group" in which one comes to belong, at least symbolically, may consist of a character or set of characters with whom one interacts through identification, such as through a movie or television series. This may be especially true if the behavior helps the character achieve an attractive goal, such as easing distress, gaining the attention of others, or gaining status within their peer group.

Social Learning Theory

Social learning theory, most commonly associated with Albert Bandura (1977), suggests that when presented with an ambiguous situation, individuals imitate actions they have witnessed others perform in the past. The classic example, based on Bandura's early experimental tests, showed that after watching a more mature person engage in violent behavior toward a doll, children in the experimental group were significantly more likely to subsequently behave aggressively toward the doll, even if the reason for the model's behavior was unclear or the aggression was unprovoked. Media, social learning theory holds, is a particularly potent force in behavior because merely observing what others do, particularly when the others are similar to the observer, can affect later behavioral choices. The ability to visualize and carry out actions that one has witnessed others engage in may ultimately determine behavior, particularly in situations in which behavioral options are ambiguous, such as while experiencing affective distress. This is true even when the original purpose for engaging in the viewed behavior is unclear because it is the contextual, visceral similarities between the observed and observer that forge the behavioral association.

Disinhibition and Script Theories

Disinhibition theory (Freedman, 1982) suggests that behaviors are spread because seeing another individual perform a considered action reduces the inhibition to perform it. Like social learning theory, disinhibition theory suggests that observing others engage in a behavior renders it more possible or conceivable. This is particularly true if an individual is conflicted about performing a certain behavior but sees another complete it successfully or with positive results. For example, in the scene from *Thirteen* described at the beginning of this chapter, observing NSSI as both painless and an effective means of quickly reducing anxiety may lower viewer inhibitions to trying the behavior in similar circumstances. The staging of the scene as one likening self-injury to an effective drug—even if its effectiveness is only temporarily—may contribute to the disinhibition effect.

Similarly, *script theory* dictates that individuals are more likely to repeat a behavior, or script, when a previous use of the behavior was successful (Albeson, 1976). Scripts represent actions, participants, and physical objects that come to represent a narrative to explain perceptions and behaviors. Script theory would predict that individuals adopt behaviors not only from observed models but also from storylines. Although applicable to unidirectional media experiences, such as viewing, reading, or listening to narratives inclusive of self-injury, script theory holds tremendous promise in explaining the effects of online bidirectional exchanges on offline behavior because participants may engage in *narrative reinforcement* (Whitlock et al., 2007), which evolves out of coconstruction of stories that essentially explain and justify self-injury linked behavioral choices—for better and worse—through interaction with others using similar scripts. Both disinhibition and script theories help to explain the desensitization and normalization of behavior that empirical studies of aggression document. Similarly, they suggest that when self injury is depicted as painless, effective, and common, inhibition may be lowered and scripts which support its value adopted.

Conclusion

The evidence reviewed in this chapter suggests that individuals vulnerable to the acquisition and maintenance of NSSI are likely to encounter both a means of exposure and multiple opportunities to experience self-injury related images, symbols, or stories, by either self-selection or chance. Uni- and bidirectional forms of media may serve as vectors for the introduction and contagion of self-injury. Indeed, the empirical data presented, although methodologically limited, support this assumption. These same processes may reinforce the behavior among those already engaging in NSSI. In light of the many mechanisms through which media influences behavior, the existence of both means and likelihood of exposure is concerning and has important implications for clinicians and researchers.

Clinical Implications

The perception that a behavior is common and rational may ultimately render treatment or intervention more difficult. Similarly, identification with individuals known or believed to engage in NSSI through social modeling or actual exchange, such as that provided through the Internet, may couple the need for belonging to a community of like-minded others who engage in NSSI. Even among individuals committed to ceasing the behavior, consistent and easy access to self-injury scripts and images in media may interfere with recovery. There are several clinical implications that follow from this review.

First, media- and Internet-use histories should be taken as part of intake and risk assessment procedures. When high use of either is detected, integration of periodic assessment and behavioral impact question routes similar to those described for the Internet (Whitlock et al., 2007) may be warranted. Lines of questioning will be most germane to treatment when they assess the degree and nature of media exposure or participation, as in the case of Internet communities, as well as the nature and magnitude of the impact on behavior.

Second, media and Internet use may introduce and reinforce self-injurious behavior through a variety of mechanisms: (a) identification of and fraternization with like-minded others; (b) behavior modeling; and (c) inclusion of scripts, sounds, or images that introduce or reinforce personal self-injury narratives. As evident in empirical studies linking media to aggression and suicide, the impact of uni- and bidirectional media is likely to be amplified when images are both plentiful and associated with high-profile individuals, such as celebrities. Assessing the mechanisms through which clients are influenced by media will assist in deciding appropriate therapeutic approaches and media-use recommendations.

Empirical Implications

Research on the relationship between media and self-injury behavior is scant. However, because uni- and bidirectional media modalities are potent vectors for the spread of ideas and behaviors, it is critical to advance understanding of the means through which they may be encouraging adoption or maintenance of the behavior. Although we present here empirical evidence that media representations of self-injury are increasingly available, it is not clear to what extent these representations influence self-injurious behavior of viewers and participants. Nor is it clear how interventions designed to moderate the relationship between media or Internet use and self-injury might most effectively do so. Well-designed empirical studies aimed at investigating the nature and magnitude of the relationship between media exposure to self-injury are needed. Such studies would focus on the effects of media and Internet use on NSSI and the extent to which these effects vary by media type and exposure.

EVALUATING THE AUTHOR'S ARGUMENTS:

The authors of this selection, Janis Whitlock, Amanda Purington, and Marina Gershkovich, maintain that the rate of self-injury among youths is likely linked to the increase in media images of self-injury over the past several years. However, they stop short of claiming that the media actually cause self-harming behavior. By way of comparison, they point to research showing that aggression is influenced by images of violence in the media. Is this a good comparison? Why or why not? How would you explain the difference between *causing* and *contributing* to an action?

References

Abelson, R. P. (1976). Script processing in attitude formation and decision-making. In J. S. Carroll & J. W. Payne (Eds.), *Cognition and social behavior* (pp. 35–45). Oxford, England: Erlbaum.

Bandura, A. (1977). *Social learning theory*. Englewood Cliffs, NJ: Prentice-Hall.

Becker, K., Mayer, M., Nagenborg, M., El-Faddagh, M., & Schmidt, M. H. (2004). Parasuicide online: Can suicide websites trigger suicidal behaviour in predisposed adolescents? *Nordic Journal of Psychiatry*, 58, 111–114.

Beller, T. (1998, August). Hollywood's freaky it girl and hello, nasty? *SPIN*, 14, 78–82,149.

Beva, T., Chasin, L., Fellner, L., Hunter, H. (Producer), & Hardwick, C. (Director). (2003). *Thirteen* [Motion picture]. United States: Michael London Productions.

Borzekowski, D. L. G., Fobil, J. N., & Asante, K. O. (2006). Online access by adolescents in Accra: Ghanaian teens' use of the Internet for health information. *Developmental Psychology*, 42, 450–458.

Bronfenbrenner, U. (1979). *The ecology of human development.* Cambridge, MA: Harvard University Press.

Brown, J. D., L'Engle, K. L., Pardun, C. J., Guo, G., Kenneavy, K., & Jackson, C. (2006). Sexy media matter: Exposure to sexual content in music, movies, television, and magazines predicts Black and White adolescents' sexual behavior. *Pediatrics*, 117, 1018–1027.

Brumberg, J. J. (2006, December). Are we facing an epidemic of self-injury? *The Chronicle Review.* Retrieved February 4, 2007, from http://chronicle.com/cgi-bin/printable.cgi?article=http://chronicle.com/weekly/v53/il6/16b00601.htm.

Bushman, B. J., & Huesmann, L. R. (2006). Short-term and long-term effects of violent media on aggression in children and adults. *Archives of Pediatrics & Adolescent Medicine*, 160, 348–352.

Center for Communication and Social Policy. (1998). *National Television Violence Study 3.* Thousand Oaks, CA: Sage.

Conroy, T., Sheffield, R., Touré, Lipsky, D., Goodell, J., Healy, M., et al. (1998, August 20). Hot actress: Christina Ricci. *Rolling Stone*, 793, 74–75.

Cook, D. E., Kestenbaum, C., Honaker, L. M., Ratcliffe Anderson, E., American Academy of Family Physicians, & American Psychiatric Association. (2000, July 26). *Joint statement on the impact of entertainment violence on children: Congressional Public Health Summit.* Retrieved April 5, 2008, from http://www.aap.org/advocacy/releases/jstmtevc.htm.

Diamond, J. (1999, January). Behind the scenes with Christina Ricci. *Mademoiselle*, 100–101,128.

Durkheim E. (1997). *Suicide.* New York: The Free Press. (Original work published 1897).

Escobar-Chaves, S. L., Tortolero, S. R., Markham, C. M., Low, B. J., Eitel, P., & Thickstun, P. (2005). Impact of the media on adolescent sexual attitudes and behaviors. *Pediatrics*, 116, 303–326.

Freedman, J. L. (1982). Theories of contagion as they relate to mass psychogenic illness. In M. J. Colligan, J. W. Pennebaker, & L. R. Murphy (Eds.), *Mass psychogenic illness* (pp. 171–182). Hillsdale, NJ: Erlbaum.

Galley, M. (2003). Student self-harm: Silent school crisis. *Education Week*, 3, 2.

Gould, M. S. (2001). Suicide and the media. *Annals of the New York Academy of Sciences*, 932, 200–221.

Gould, M. S., Jamieson, P., & Romer, D. (2003). Media contagion and suicide among the young. *American Behavioral Scientist*, 46, 1269–1284.

Hampton, K. N., & Wellman, D. (2003). Neighboring in Netville: How the Internet supports community and social capital in a wired suburb. *City & Community*, 2, 277–311.

Heath, C. (1993, May). Johnny Depp—Portrait of the oddest as a young man. *Details*, 88–95, 166, 168.

Heath, C. (1998a, January 22). Fiona, the caged bird sings. *Rolling Stone*. Retrieved July 1, 2007, from http://sites.uol.com.br/diogo henriques/artigos/rs01-98.html.

Heath, C. (1998b, November). The love song of Marilyn Manson. *Guitar School*. Retrieved July 1, 2007, from http://www.basetend encies.com/press/RollingStone98.html.

Heath, C. (2001, July 5). Blood sugar sex magic. *Rolling Stone*, 872, 68–79, 156.

Heath, C. (2004, October). The wild one. *GQ*. Retrieved July 1, 2007, from http://www.colinfarrellfansite.com/gallery/thumbnails. php ?album=128&page=l

Heath, N. L., Toste, J. R., & Beettam, E. (2006). "I am not well-equipped": High school teachers' perceptions of self-injury. *Canadian Journal of School Psychology*, 21, 73–92.

Holmes reveals self-harm ordeal. (2005, May 29). *BBC Sport*. Retrieved July 1, 2007, from http://news.bbc.co.uk/sportl/hi/ath letics/4590655.stm.

Huesmann, L. R., Moise-Titus, J., Podolski, C.-L., & Eron, L. D. (2003). Longitudinal relations between children's exposure to TV violence and their aggressive and violent behavior in young adult: 1977–1992. *Developmental Psychology*, 39, 201–221.

Jackson, L. A., vonEye, A., Biocca, F. A., Barbatsis, G., Zhao, Y., & Fitzgerald, H. E. (2006). How does home Internet use influence the academic performance of low-income children? *Developmental Psychology*, 42, 429–435.

Johnson, J. G., Cohen, P., Smailes, E. M., Kasen, S., & Brook, J. S. (2002, March 29). Television viewing and aggressive behavior during adolescence and adulthood. *Science*, 295, 2468–2471.

Kavanaugh, A., & Patterson, S. J. (2001). The impact of community computer networks on social capital and community involvement. *American Behavioral Scientist*, 45, 496–509.

Kublin, K. S., Wetherby, A. M., Crais, E. R., & Prizant, B. M. (1998). Using dynamic assessment within collaborative contexts: The transition from intentional to symbolic communication. In A. M. Wetherby, S. F. Warren, & J. Reichle (Eds.), *Transitions in prelinguistic communication: Preintentional to intentional and presymbolic to symbolic* (pp. 285–312). Baltimore: Brookes Publishing.

Maerz, J. (2001, October 31). Appetite for resurrection. *SF Weekly*. Retrieved July 1, 2007, from http://www.sfweekly.com/2001-10-31/music/appetite-for-resurrection.

Marsden, P. (1998). Memetics and social contagion: Two sides of the same coin? *Journal of Memetics*, 2, 68–86.

Norris, M. L., Boydell, K. M., Pinhas, L., & Katzman, D. K. (2006). Ana and the Internet: A review of pro-anorexia websites. *International Journal of Eating Disorders*, 39, 443–447.

Paik, H., & Comstock, G. (1994). The effects of television violence on anti-social behavior: A meta-analysis. *Communication Research*, 21, 516–546.

Phillips, D. (1974). The influence of suggestion on suicide: Substantive and theoretical implication of the Werther effect. *American Sociological Review*, 39, 340–354.

Ro, R. (2000, May 30). *Garbage's Shirley Manson admits to "cutting."* Retrieved July 1, 2007, from http://www.mtv.com/news/articles/1429321/20000530/nullgarbage.jhtml.

Roberts, D. F., Foehr, U. G., & Rideout, V. (2005). *Generation M: Media in the lives of 8–18 year-olds.* Washington, DC: Henry J. Kaiser Family Foundation.

Stack, S. (2000). Media impacts on suicide: A quantitative review of 293 findings. *Social Science Quarterly,* 81, 957–971.

Turner, R. H. (1964). Collective behavior. In R. E. L. Faris (Ed.), *Handbook of modern sociology* (pp. 382–425). Chicago: Rand McNally.

Turner, R. H., & Killian, L. M. (1972). *Collective behavior.* Englewood Cliffs, NY: Prentice-Hall.

Villa 65. (1995, November). *Radio interview with Richey Edward.* Retrieved July 1, 2007, from http://articles.richeyedwards.net /dutchradionov94.html.

Vygotsky, L. (1986). *Thought and language.* Cambridge, MA: MIT Press. (Original work published 1934).

Weiss, P. (1998, October). The Love issue. *SPIN.* Retrieved July 1, 2007, from http://www.angelfire.com/hi/barbiesdead/spin98.html.

Welsh, P. (June 28, 2004). Students' scars point to emotional pain. *USA Today,* p. 11a.

Whitlock, J. L., Eells, G., Cummings, N., & Purington, A. (in press). Non-suicidal self-injury on college campuses: Mental health provider assessment of prevalence and need. *Journal of College Student Psychotherapy.*

Whitlock, J. L., Lader, W., & Conterio, K. (2007). The role of virtual communities in self-injury treatment: Clinical considerations. *Journal of Clinical Psychology: In Session,* 63, 1135–1143.

Whitlock, J. L., Powers, J. L., & Eckenrode, J. (2006). The virtual cutting edge: The Internet and adolescent self-injury. *Developmental Psychology,* 42, 407–417.

Wurtzel, E. (1994). *Prozac nation.* New York: Berkley.

Ybarra, M. L., & Mitchell, K. J. (2005). Exposure to Internet pornography among children and adolescents: A national survey. *CyberPsychology & Behavior,* 8, 473–486.

A Variety of Factors Can Cause People to Injure Themselves

"There's no one reason why one person self-harms and another doesn't."

Julia Pearlman

Numerous factors can lead to self-harming behavior, writes Julia Pearlman in the following viewpoint. Self-injury can affect anyone, regardless of background—although some groups of people are more prone to the behavior, such as troubled youths, prisoners, and those who abuse substances. People with mental health problems are at higher risk of self-injury, although self-harm is not always a sign of mental illness. The author explains that the reasons people engage in self-harm include a need to relieve emotional tension, a way to communicate pain, and a desire to punish themselves. Pearlman writes for TheSite.org, a United Kingdom–based online guide to life for sixteen- to twenty-five-year-olds.

There's no one reason why one person self-harms and another doesn't. Some people may even self-harm and have no awareness of what they're doing, known as dissociation. Most of all, it's often the result of deep emotional pain.

Self-Harm Can Affect Anyone

There's no such thing as a typical person who self-harms. It can affect anyone of any age, background or race, regardless of whether they are an extrovert or an introvert. In fact, a 2012 survey of young people showed that 86% of respondents said they had injured themselves, with over half saying they did it regularly.

"Around friends and the public you may seem OK, but it's not like you want to go around looking depressed and feeling sorry for yourself," says JD, 17. You feel different inside to how you show yourself on the outside and you do put on a bit of a front, so you can't just look at someone and say 'they self-harm'."

Some young people self-harm on a regular basis, while others do it just once or a few times. For some people it's part of coping with a specific problem and they stop once the problem is resolved. Other people self-harm for years whenever certain kinds of pressures and problems arise.

Vulnerable Groups

Some people may be more likely to self-harm than others. These include:

- Girls and young women (although recent research shows that the difference between men and women is less obvious than previously thought)

- Young people aged between 15 and 25 years old
- People who live in residential care or secure institutions
- Gay, bisexual, transgender men and women
- Asian women
- People who are dependent on alcohol or street drugs

Overall, women are more likely to self-harm than men—this is most evident in adolescence. However, men are more likely to self-injure and women are more likely to self-poison. The National Institute of Clinical Excellence (NICE) has outlined other groups in society that may be more prone to self-harm, including people with learning disabilities, and prisoners—as many as 10% of whom will self-harm during their term.

FAST FACT

The Mayo Clinic reports that unstable living conditions such as unemployment or divorce may foster self-harming behavior.

Research also suggests that drinking a lot of alcohol can significantly increase the risk of self-harm in young people who are already feeling stressed or depressed—up to half of people who are seen in A&E [accident and emergency rooms] following self-harm will have used alcohol.

What Causes Self-Harm?

If you've got mental health problems, such as depression or severe anxiety, you have a higher risk of self-harming. But if you do self-harm, it doesn't necessarily mean that you have a serious mental illness—it may just be that you're feeling alone, isolated, stressed, frustrated, or angry about issues out of your control. Such issues might include one or more of the following:

- Low self-esteem
- Poor body image
- Bullying or discrimination
- Unwanted pregnancy
- A serious illness that affects the way you feel about yourself
- Worries over sexuality
- Cultural/racial difficulties

- Feelings of rejection, lack of love and affection by parents or carers
- Parents getting divorced/family breakdown and conflict
- Physical, sexual or emotional abuse
- Domestic violence
- A bereavement
- Work pressures
- Money worries
- Depression
- The self-harm or suicide of someone close to you
- Isolation and loneliness
- Anxiety
- Drug and alcohol misuse
- Relationship problems

Some people harm themselves because they don't know how else to cope with pressures from family, school and peer groups. Extreme feelings such as fear, anger, guilt, shame, helplessness, self-hatred, unhappiness, depression or despair can build up over time. When these feelings become unbearable, self-harm can be a way of dealing with them.

Bullying is just one of the many factors that can lead to self-injury, according to the author.

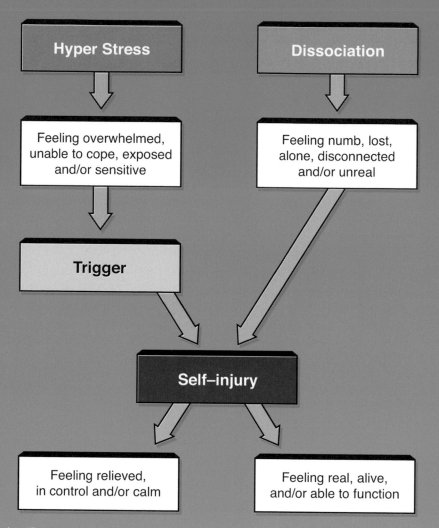

Precursors to Self–Injury

Hyper Stress → Feeling overwhelmed, unable to cope, exposed and/or sensitive → **Trigger**

Dissociation → Feeling numb, lost, alone, disconnected and/or unreal

Self–injury

Feeling relieved, in control and/or calm

Feeling real, alive, and/or able to function

Reasons young people have given for their self-harm include:

• When the level of emotional pressure becomes too high it acts as a safety valve—a way of relieving the tension
• Cutting makes the blood take away the bad feelings
• Pain can make you feel more alive when feeling numb or dead inside

- Punishing oneself in response to feelings of shame or guilt
- When it's too difficult to talk to anyone, it's a form of communication about unhappiness and a way of acknowledging the need for help
- Self-harm gives a sense of control that's missing elsewhere in life

Some people self-harm with the intention of ending their life or they may be unsure about whether they want to survive, for example, taking an overdose and leaving it to fate to decide the outcome.

Sorting Self-Harm Fact from Fiction

Many organisations and health professionals are calling for more information in hospitals and schools to tackle the stigma around the issue of self-harming, which can often put young people off seeking help and advice. In the Samaritans' [a British charity for those in emotional distress or at risk of suicide] report *Youth Matters—A Cry for Help*, 43% of young people knew someone who has self-harmed, but one-in-four had no idea what to say to a friend who was self-harming or feeling suicidal. Most worryingly, 41% of young people believed that self-harm is selfish and 55% think that it is stupid.

Even though self-harm can provide immediate, temporary relief it does not deal with the issues underlying the distress. Often it's not easy for someone to admit that they have a problem, let alone to confide in anyone about what they are doing. If you're worried about self-harm in any way, there are lots of people who can offer you help and guidance so you don't have to deal with it on your own.

EVALUATING THE AUTHOR'S ARGUMENTS:

Many health-care providers feel that information on self-harm needs to be made more widely available in hospitals and schools to lessen the stigma surrounding the behavior, author Julia Pearlman points out. Do you think that this would encourage more self-injurers to seek help? Why or why not?

Chapter 3

How Can Self-Injurers Be Helped?

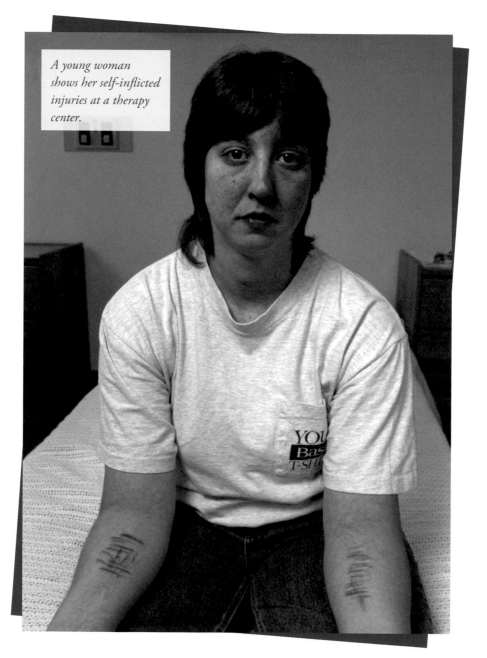

A young woman shows her self-inflicted injuries at a therapy center.

Therapy Helps Self-Injurers

Miranda Sweet and Janis Whitlock

"One goal of treatment is to recognize the impulse to harm oneself as a clue that something bigger is going on."

In the following viewpoint Miranda Sweet and Janis Whitlock outline the aims and approaches of two different types of treatment for self-injury: individual therapy and family therapy. The main goals of both types of therapy are to help self-injurers understand why they have the impulse to harm themselves and to identify healthier ways of coping with emotional turmoil, the authors explain. In individual therapy, a mental health professional will tailor the treatment to the client's needs. In family therapy, the authors describe, the therapist works with each member of a family—and sometimes the client's friends as well—to provide a safe place for sharing thoughts and feelings and to help the family better understand what triggers self-harming behavior. Sweet and Whitlock are both researchers with the Cornell Research Program on Self-Injurious Behavior in Adolescents and Young Adults in Ithaca, New York.

Miranda Sweet and Janis Whitlock, "Therapy: What to Expect," Cornell Research Program on Self-Injurious Behavior, 2010, pp. 1–4. Copyright © 2010 by Cornell Research Program on Self-Injurious Behavior in Adolescents and Young Adults. All rights reserved. Reproduced by permission.

AS YOU READ, CONSIDER THE FOLLOWING QUESTIONS:
1. What does a therapist typically do during the first therapy session, according to the authors?
2. In the authors' view, why do people often feel worse before they begin to feel better while undergoing therapy?
3. Why is it important for each family-therapy participant to understand what can trigger self-injuring behavior, according to the authors?

W*hat are the goals of individual therapy for the treatment of self-injury?* While stopping self-injury is a main goal, before approaching this, the individual first needs to gain a better understanding of the functions of his or her self-injury. According to Wendy Lader, co-founder of S.A.F.E. Alternatives [Self Abuse Finally Ends], one goal of treatment is to recognize the impulse to harm oneself as a clue that something bigger is going on. Each time the individual has an urge to self-injure, he or she should ask him/herself, "Why at this moment do I have this impulse? What am I trying to push away or not feel?" This will help the person identify common triggers and underlying issues at work. This is the first step in coming up with more positive ways of coping. Becoming aware of self-injury triggers, motives behind them, and productive strategies for resolving underlying issues are typically central goals of treatment.

I am ready for therapy. What is the first step? If you are in touch with someone who may know of a counselor, therapist, psychologist, or other mental health professional in your area who might be a good fit for you, asking for a recommendation is a good first step. Most communities have listings of local therapists with brief summaries of their areas of expertise as well—even web-based searches of mental health providers in your region are likely to pull up something useful. For help finding someone with particular expertise in self-injury you can visit the S.A.F.E. Alternatives website. There you will find a thorough overview of how to find a therapist specifically for the treatment of self-injury. . . .

The First Session

I have made the appointment. What can I expect during the first session? A new client should show up at least 10 minutes before the scheduled time to fill out necessary paperwork, including a form which must be signed to consent to the therapeutic relationship. Though a therapy session is generally called an "hour," the typical appointment length is 50 minutes. At the beginning of the session, the therapist will usually go over office policies (cancellation policy, confidentiality, etc.) and answer any questions you might have about the paperwork and process. Although this all takes time, these steps are an important part of building a trusting relationship.

The therapist will typically begin by asking you to describe specifically why you are seeking therapy (if this has not been thoroughly covered during the phone call or initial meeting). This is often followed by a series of questions designed to better understand your life story as it relates to the present issues with which you are struggling including, but not limited to, self-injury. Because it is common for individuals who struggle with one negative behavior, such as self-injury, to also be experiencing or practicing other negative feelings or behaviors, the therapist is likely to ask about other behaviors, thoughts, and feelings as well. He or she will also ask about your life in general. This may include questions about your childhood, education, past and current relationships with family and friends, and school or work life. It will likely take more than just the initial appointment to complete this history, but the therapist uses this information to come up with a treatment plan tailored to your particular life and situation. In the last few minutes of the session, the therapist usually summarizes his or her understanding of what you have shared and reviews any agreements you may have made together. The therapist will probably ask you again how you feel after the first session and you may decide on a schedule for regular appointments at this time if the relationship seems like it is a good fit.

Each Individual Is Unique

What can I expect in subsequent sessions? The initial appointments are necessary so that the therapist can gather information and begin to establish rapport with the client, but after this, the real work begins! Usually, appointments are scheduled on a weekly basis, but more frequent or extended appointments may be necessary. Each person's experience of therapy is unique so it is difficult to describe what the nature of one's specific therapeutic relationship will be like. Likewise, the course of treatment is different for each individual and is based on his or her personal goals and issues. Keep in mind that research shows the single most curative factor in therapy is the *relationship* between the therapist and the client. It is essential that one honestly shares any feelings or issues one may have about how the course of treatment is going with one's therapist in order to maximize the benefits one will receive from therapy. Be aware that it is common to feel *worse* before one starts to feel better, and this is not a reason to stop therapy. This happens because sometimes certain problems may surface for the first time; this can be painful but it is also a clear sign that one is making progress! . . .

Family Therapy

What is family therapy? Family therapy is focused on working with all individuals in a family (this sometimes includes extended families or even friends) to create a more supportive environment for the individual family member with whom the therapist is primarily working.

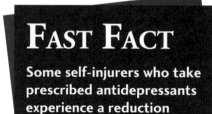

FAST FACT

Some self-injurers who take prescribed antidepressants experience a reduction in the urge to hurt themselves.

Family therapy capitalizes on the important role that family relationships play in overall psychological wellbeing. Because of this, family therapy typically focuses on identifying and addressing patterns between family members that lead to the negative thoughts, feelings, or actions of one or more members of the family. It is intended to provide a safe place for family members to share thoughts and feelings that they might not otherwise share and also to practice new ways of communicating and interacting.

What family therapy is not. Family therapy is *not* about playing the blame game; rather, all family members are encouraged to identify steps that they can take to create a home environment that is healthy for everyone involved. Family therapy is not about making assumptions about the processes in one's family. No one family pattern "breeds" self-injury.

Why use family therapy to treat self-injury? When working with someone who self-injures, the main goal of inviting family members to

In individual therapy, self-injurers attempt to gain a better understanding of why they are compelled to hurt themselves.

participate in therapy is to explore how family patterns may be inadvertently supporting the behavior. Since self-injury is often a way of expressing emotion without words, family therapy sessions are also intended to increase the capacity of families to communicate honestly and openly about what works and does not work in their interactions. Since it is common for individuals who struggle with self-injury to come from families who find sharing emotions difficult, the family therapist can be very helpful in helping all family members express thoughts and emotions to one another. The therapist also often has useful suggestions for improving communication in everyday life. The family therapy sessions can also be used to identify family strengths and strategies for using them in new ways when faced with family challenges.

Common Myths About Therapy

- Only crazy people see therapists.

- Therapy is self-indulgent or only for "weak" people.

- The past is the past, and you should be over it already.

- Someone who does not know me cannot help me.

- Therapy is too expensive.

- My therapist will tell me what to do.

- Therapy does not work or it will take years to sort out my issues.

- Once a person has completed therapy, there is no way it will ever be needed again.

Triggering Dynamics

Involving the family may help a person to feel less "invisible" in his or her family system. Also, working together with the individual helps the parents and other family members better understand what triggers self-injury episodes. When family members begin to understand what triggers an act of self-injury, they can work together to develop more effective and productive family strategies for dealing with potentially triggering family dynamics. The goal here is not to avoid self-injury triggers but to learn how to work with them differently as a family. Helping family members become aware of triggering dynamics increases opportunities to practice new ways of coping and relating individually and collective.

What can I expect in a family therapy session? Family therapy is generally short in duration, lasting an average of 12 sessions. It is also typically highly goal-oriented. In the first sessions, the family therapist will observe how family members communicate and interact with one another and will also take note of non-verbal cues about the quality of family relationships. The therapist may ask about each family member's expectations for therapy in order to outline goals for treatment. The therapist is also likely to ask about strategies family members have tried in the past to increase positive exchange, support, and communication. Family members can expect some education about self-injury and the process of recovery, particularly if the topic is new to them. In following sessions, clients are asked to provide feedback to the therapist about the quality of these family relationships and generally how the process of change is progressing. . . .

Working on Recovery

How does a family therapy session compare to an individual therapy session? As with individual therapy, a family therapist will devote the first session to understanding the meaning of self-injury within the family context with a particular focus on understanding the role family dynamics play in triggering or reinforcing the self-injurious behavior. By soliciting the perspectives of all family members present, the therapist will gain a much deeper understanding about how the individual's self-injury fits in the family system. This understanding will be central in identifying strategies for recovery.

EVALUATING THE AUTHOR'S ARGUMENTS:

Miranda Sweet and Janis Whitlock describe two different modes of professional treatment for self-injury: individual therapy and family therapy. What are the advantages of each type of therapy? Do you think one type of therapy would be more effective than the other for a self-injurer? Explain your answer.

Deliberate Self-Harm

ReachOut.com

> *"It may take time, but it's important to remember that you can move to a happier and healthier outlook."*

ReachOut.com is a web-based emergency help line and information service in Australia for youths who have questions about health, cultural differences, sexuality, and other issues. In the following viewpoint ReachOut.com offers several self-help strategies that can help people reduce or stop self-injuring. The suggestions include activities that help to vent feelings and release energy, as well as substitute behaviors, such as squeezing ice or eating a very spicy food. ReachOut.com emphasizes, however, that it is important for a self-harmer to seek support from a friend or a health-care professional.

AS YOU READ, CONSIDER THE FOLLOWING QUESTIONS:
1. According to the author, when are health-care professionals required to report confidential information about a patient?
2. What kinds of relaxation techniques help to release energy and feelings, in the author's view?
3. According to the author, why is it important for a self-injurer to eat well and exercise?

Although it might seem hard, it's important that you reach out to someone who can help you find healthier, positive alternatives to alleviate the pain you feel inside. It may take time, but it's important to remember that you can move to a happier and healthier outlook.

Speaking to someone about your self-harm might be hard, and it's important to trust the person you're speaking with.

If you're having a hard time talking about what you're going through, you might start with sentences such as "Right now, I'm feeling . . ."; "I think it started when . . ."; "I've been feeling this for . . ."; "My sleep has been . . ."; "Lately school/work has been . . ."

Like any relationship, building trust with your counselor, psychologist or psychiatrist may take time and it is important you find someone you feel comfortable with. This may mean seeing several people before finding the one that you "click" with.

If there is a family member you feel comfortable telling, it might be helpful for you to have their support in finding a counselor that is right for you. It's likely that the person you feel comfortable telling will already be worried about you and will be relieved to have the opportunity to listen and help.

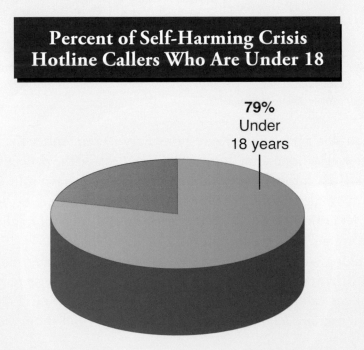

Percent of Self-Harming Crisis Hotline Callers Who Are Under 18

79%
Under
18 years

Taken from: Boys Town. "Cutting and Self–Injury: We Can Help." Parenting.org, 2012.

The author suggests calling for crisis counseling as a way of coping with crisis or suicidal thoughts. Two organizations recommended by the author are National Suicide Prevention Lifeline or the Boys Town National Hotline.

If you don't get a positive response, try to remember that it's not because you've done something wrong, but because the person you have told may not know how to respond to what you have told them, or might not understand much about deliberate self-harm. Don't give up! Either try again or speak to someone else you think you might receive a more supportive response from.

If talking with someone is too overwhelming, an alternative is to e-mail or write down what you want to say. Otherwise, a first step might be to call the National Suicide Prevention Lifeline (1-800-273-8255) if you are feeling in crisis or having suicidal thoughts, or the

Boys Town National Hotline (1-800-448-3000)—both of which are free, 24-hour help lines.

If you or a friend are harming yourselves, it's also important that you take care of the injuries caused and if necessary, seek medical help through your doctor or, if it's serious, a hospital's emergency department. You might also want to check out the Get Help section of ReachOut for more information about who can help.

In most situations, doctors and other health professionals must keep your information confidential. However, they are required to report information they receive if they have serious concerns about your safety. See the Confidentiality fact sheet for more info.

Coping Without Harming Yourself

Along with support from a friend, family member or health professional, it might also be helpful to write a list of alternative strategies to self-harm for managing your emotions.

If you feel like you want to harm yourself, there are a number of things that you can try to distract yourself until the feelings become more manageable. If you can, make sure that you're around other people and remove any sharp objects from the area.

FAST FACT

Some counselors suggest that self-harmers wear rubber bands on their wrists, arms, or legs and flick them instead of cutting themselves.

Some ideas for releasing energy or feelings include:

- Choose to put off harming yourself until you've spoken to someone else or waited for 15 minutes. See if you can extend it for another 15 minutes beyond that, continue to do it again until the feelings pass;
- Write in a journal. You might try to use an online journal that is password protected;
- Exercise. Go for a run or walk in the park to use up excess energy;
- Play video games. This might be a good way to distract yourself and help until the anxiety passes;
- Yell or sing at the top of your lungs on your own or to music. You might do this into a pillow if you don't want other people in the house to hear;

- Draw or write in red pen over your body (instead of cutting);
- Use Relaxation techniques. Activities like yoga or meditation are often helpful in reducing anxiety;
- Cry. Crying is a healthy and normal way to express your sadness or frustrations;
- Talk to someone, like a trusted friend, or call a help line like those mentioned above—Lifeline (1-800-273-8255) or Boys Town help line (1-800-448-3000).

Alternatives to Deliberate Self-Harm
If the above suggestions don't help and you still feel the need to self harm, there are a number of things that you can do that won't cause injury like:

- Punching a pillow or punching bag;
- Squeezing ice cubes until your fingers go numb;
- Eating a chili, or something really spicy;
- Taking a cold shower;
- Putting vapor rub under your nose (it stings and makes you cry);
- Waxing your legs (or getting them waxed).

Take Care of Yourself
It's important to eat well, exercise and be kind to yourself. While not a solution in itself, doing all these things contribute to a higher sense of self-worth, increased stability of moods, and a general better sense of well being—making you feel more happy on the outside and the inside.

EVALUATING THE AUTHOR'S ARGUMENTS:

The author, ReachOut.com, suggests several activities to engage in as alternatives to self-harm, such as squeezing ice cubes and drawing in red on one's body. The author emphasizes, however, that these activities are for emergency use only. Why do you think ReachOut.com warns against resorting to these activities too frequently?

Self-Harm and Trauma: Research Findings

Laura E. Gibson and Tina Crenshaw

"The group that received the self-harm CBT [cognitive behavioral therapy] showed a significant reduction in self-harming behaviors."

Self-harm may begin in adolescence or early adulthood, and it often reflects abuse or trauma in childhood, Laura E. Gibson and Tina Crenshaw state in the following viewpoint. A high percentage of people who suffer from PTSD (post-traumatic stress disorder) also suffer from self-harm, they say. Often self-harmers are embarrassed about or ashamed to discuss their self-harming actions, say the authors. They may try to hide their scars and avoid seeking psychological or medical treatment. The psychological treatment known as cognitive behavioral therapy, or CBT, has had success in significantly reducing self-harming behaviors, report Gibson and Crenshaw. Psychopharmacological treatments might be helpful in reducing self-harm behaviors, but use of such treatments are complicated by the fact that self-harm can occur with other psychological problems. Gibson and Crenshaw are researchers for the National

Laura E. Gibson and Tina Crenshaw, "Self-Harm and Trauma: Research Findings," National Center for PTSD, Professional Section: Information on Trauma and PTSD Researchers, Providers, & Helpers, US Department of Veterans Affairs, 2012.

Center for PTSD, the center of excellence for research and education on the prevention, understanding, and treatment of PTSD. Although it provides no direct clinical care, its purpose is to improve the well-being and understanding of American veterans.

AS YOU READ, CONSIDER THE FOLLOWING QUESTIONS:
1. What percentage of individuals diagnosed with PTSD also engaged in self-harm, according the sample of psychiatric outpatients mentioned by the authors?
2. What four factors in childhood are common causes of self-harm later in life, as stated in the viewpoint?
3. Why is there is no consensus regarding whether or not psychiatric medications should be used in relation to self-harm behaviors, according to Gibson and Crenshaw?

What Is Self-Harm? Self-harm refers to the deliberate, direct destruction of body tissue. Other terms for self-harm include "parasuicide," "self-mutilation," "self-injury," "self-abuse," "cutting," or "self-inflicted violence." When someone engages in self-harm, they may have a variety of intentions; these are discussed below. However, the person's intention is not to kill himself or herself.

Self-harm tends to begin in adolescence or early adulthood. While some people may engage in self-harm a few times and then stop, others engage in it frequently and have great difficulty stopping the behavior (1). Self-harm is related to trauma in that those who engage in self-harm are likely to have experienced abuse in childhood (2–6).

How Common Is Self-Harm?

The rates of self-harm revealed through research vary tremendously, depending on how researchers pose their questions about this behavior. Estimates of lifetime self-harm prevalence in the general population range from 2.2% to 6% (2). In samples of students, the rates are higher, ranging from 13% to 35% (2).

In studies that have compared general population samples to clinical samples, the rates of self-harm were higher in the clinical samples (2–3). Within clinical samples, those with a diagnosis of PTSD report higher rates of self-harm than do those without PTSD (7). In one sample of psychiatric outpatients, as many as 60% of those with a diagnosis of PTSD reported harming themselves in the previous three months (7).

Characteristics of Self-Harmers

A systematic review of the literature on correlates of self-harm found that self-harmers, as compared to others, have more frequent and more negative emotions such as anxiety, depression, and aggressiveness. Links between self-harm and dissociation, low emotional expressivity, and low self-esteem have also been found (2). The evidence on whether self-harm is more common in females or males is mixed (2–3, 7).

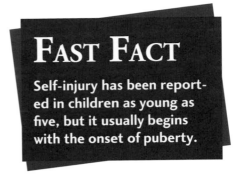

FAST FACT

Self-injury has been reported in children as young as five, but it usually begins with the onset of puberty.

Individuals who self-harm appear to have higher rates of PTSD and other psychological problems (1, 4–6). Self-harm may be most often related to trauma exposure in childhood rather than adulthood (2–3). A number of studies (2–6) have found that individuals who engage in self-harm report unusually high rates of histories of:

- Childhood sexual abuse
- Childhood physical abuse
- Emotional neglect
- Insecure attachment
- Prolonged separation from caregivers

Childhood sexual abuse appears especially frequently in the histories of those who self-harm (2). In one sample of individuals who self-harmed, 93% reported a history of childhood sexual abuse (3). Some research has looked at whether particular characteristics of childhood sexual abuse place individuals at greater risk for engaging in self-harm as adults. More severe, more frequent, or a longer duration of sexual abuse was associated with an increased risk of engaging in self-harm in one's adult years (8–9).

Why Do People Engage in Self-Harm?

While there are many theories about why individuals harm themselves, the answer to this question may vary from individual to individual (10–11). One study specifically examined the reasons given for the behavior in a sample of self-harmers (3). The top two reasons were "To distract yourself from painful feelings" and "To punish yourself." When factor analysis was applied the responses, nine factors were found:

- Decrease dissociative symptoms, especially depersonalization and numbing.
- Reduce stress and tension.
- Block upsetting memories and flashbacks.
- Demonstrate a need for help.
- Ensure safety and self-protection.
- Express and release distress.
- Reduce anger.
- Disfigure self as punishment.
- Hurt self in lieu of others.

How Is Self-Harm Treated?

Self-harm is a problem that many people are embarrassed or ashamed to discuss. Often, individuals try to hide their self-harm behaviors and are very reluctant to seek needed psychological or even medical treatment.

Psychological Treatments. Because self-harm is often associated with other psychological problems, it tends to be treated under the umbrella of a co-occurring disorder like PTSD, substance abuse, or borderline personality disorder. There is evidence, however, suggesting more improvement when the self-harming behavior is the primary focus of treatment. A randomized controlled trial looked at the effects of adding a short cognitive behavioral therapy (CBT) intervention focused on self-harm to treatment as usual in a sample of self-harmers. Treatment as usual included medications or psychotherapy not specific to self-harm. The group that received the self-harm CBT showed a significant reduction in self-harming behaviors, as compared to the group receiving only treatment as usual (12).

Pharmacological Treatments. It is possible that psychopharmacological treatments would be helpful in reducing self-harm behaviors, but this has not yet been rigorously studied. As yet, there is no consensus regarding whether or not psychiatric medications should be used in relation to self-harm behaviors. This is a complicated issue to study because self-harm can occur in many different populations and co-occur with many different kinds of psychological problems.

EVALUATING THE AUTHOR'S ARGUMENTS:

The authors of this viewpoint, Laura E. Gibson and Tina Crenshaw, suggest that psychopharmacological treatments might be helpful in reducing self-harm behaviors. Review the other viewpoints in this chapter, and determine under what conditions drug therapy would be beneficial. Explain your position.

References

1. Simeon, D., & Hollander, E. (Eds.). (2001). *Self injurious behaviors: Assessment and treatment.* Washington, DC: American Psychiatric Press.
2. Fliege, H., Lee, J., Grimm, A., & Klapp, B.F. (2009). Risk factors and correlates of deliberate self-harm behavior: A systematic review. *Journal of Psychosomatic Research, 66(6),* 477–493.
3. Briere, J., & Gil, E. (1998). Self-mutilation in clinical and general population samples: Prevalence, correlates, and functions. *American Journal of Orthopsychiatry, 68(4),* 609–620.
4. Gratz, K.L., Conrad, S.D., & Roemer, L. (2002). Risk factors for deliberate self-harm among college students. *American Journal of Orthopsychiatry, 72,* 128–140.
5. Van der Kolk, B.A., Perry, J.C., & Herman, J.L. (1991). Childhood origins of self-destructive behavior. *American Journal of Psychiatry, 148,* 1665–1671.
6. Zlotnick, C., Shea, M.T., Pearlstein, T., Simpson, E., Costello, E., & Begin, A. (1996). The relationship between dissociative

symptoms, alexithymia, impulsivity, sexual abuse, and self-mutilation. *Comprehensive Psychiatry, 37,* 12–16.

7. Zlotnick, C., Mattia, J.I., & Zimmerman, M. (1999). Clinical correlates of self-mutilation in a sample of general psychiatric patients. *The Journal of Nervous and Mental Disease, 187,* 296–301.

8. Boudewyn, A.C., & Liem, J.H. (1995). Childhood sexual abuse as a precursor to depression and self-destructive behavior in adulthood. *Journal of Traumatic Stress, 8,* 445–459.

9. Turell, S.C., & Armsworth, M.W. (2000). Differentiating incest survivors who self-mutilate. *Child Abuse & Neglect, 24,* 237–249.

10. Conterio, K., & Lader, W. (1998). *Bodily harm: The breakthrough healing program for self-injurers.* New York: Hyperion.

11. Favazza, A. (1998). The coming of age of self-mutilation. *Journal of Nervous and Mental Disease, 186,* 259–268.

12. Slee, N., Garnefski, N., van der Leeden, R., Arensman, E., & Spinhoven, P. (2008). Cognitive-behavioural intervention for self-harm: Randomised controlled trial. *British Journal of Psychiatry. 192(3),* 202–211.

Self-Harming Nfld. Teen Loses Right to Refuse Treatment

"The 'best interests' of an adolescent must be taken into account when his or her competency is being assessed."

Kirk Makin

In the following viewpoint Kirk Makin reports on the case of a sixteen-year-old girl in Newfoundland (Nfld.), Canada, who has severely injured herself dozens of times. In this part of Canada, sixteen-year-olds are allowed to refuse medical and psychotherapeutic treatment if they are mentally competent. In this particular case, however, a judge ruled that the girl should be denied this right even though she is intelligent and aware. As Makin points out, the judge's intention was to send a message to health-care professionals who prefer to avoid treating difficult patients. Some self-injurers require a lot of attention and need to remain in treatment—even against their will—rather than being quickly released before their underlying problems have been addressed. Makin is a reporter for the *Globe and Mail* in Toronto, Canada.

A ruling that removes the right to make treatment decisions from a 16-year-old Newfoundland girl who compulsively consumes metal objects is being hailed as a breakthrough in protecting adolescents who harm themselves.

Lawyers familiar with the case say it provides a blueprint for reducing the number of self-harming teenagers who are shunted in and out of mental-health facilities.

In his ruling, Mr. Justice Richard LeBlanc of the Newfoundland and Labrador Supreme Court said that the girl—known as S. J. L.—is intelligent and self-aware, yet her illness prevents her from understanding that she will succeed in killing herself unless properly treated.

"To me, the lack of ability to control her urges is a manifestation of the condition that she suffers from," Judge LeBlanc said. "Death is not a desirable or necessary result of the condition she suffers from. Help is out there for her, and it is my hope that she will benefit from what is made available to her."

The girl has been held under high security at a St. John's hospital while the courtroom battle raged over her competency to refuse treatment.

Over the past two years, she had been confined, treated and then released 49 times after swallowing objects ranging from razor blades to a bread knife and a metal protractor. She has tried repeatedly to strangle herself and slit her wrists.

On nine occasions, she underwent surgery to remove objects, causing doctors to recently warn that a build-up in scar tissue indicates that she may not survive another operation.

> **FAST FACT**
>
> Many mental health advocates argue that medical personnel need training to help dispel their prejudices about self-harmers.

John Bradford, associate chief of forensic psychiatry at Royal Ottawa Hospital, applauded the ruling, saying it likely will make it harder for hospitals to manipulate diagnostic criteria in order to duck tough cases that involve self-injuring youths.

He believes too many hospital doctors release people like S. J. L. because they use up bed space, they require a great deal of attention and they are so hard to treat. To do this, doctors arbitrarily manipulate aspects of the diagnosis to make it more justifiable to send the patients on their way.

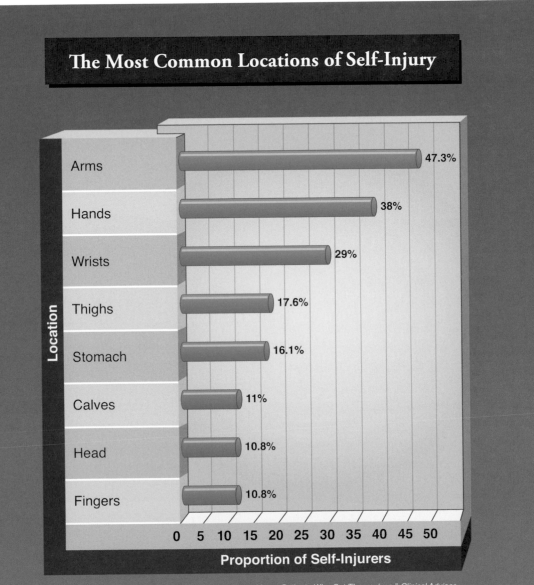

The Most Common Locations of Self-Injury

Arms — 47.3%
Hands — 38%
Wrists — 29%
Thighs — 17.6%
Stomach — 16.1%
Calves — 11%
Head — 10.8%
Fingers — 10.8%

Location

Proportion of Self-Injurers

0 5 10 15 20 25 30 35 40 45 50

Taken from: Blaise Aguirre and Brian D. Smith. "Handling Young Patients Who Cut Themselves." *Clinical Advisor*, August 2007.

"I think this was the right decision," Dr. Bradford said. "It sends a message that it wasn't helping this girl to be in this revolving door. It doesn't help hospitals either, because they can be accused of not responding properly."

David C. Day, a St. John's lawyer appointed by Judge LeBlanc to look after the child's best interests, said that the ruling establishes that the "best interests" of an adolescent must be taken into account when his or her competency is being assessed.

Robert Buckingham, a lawyer representing the girl's mother, said that the decision broke ground by taking the girl's personal views into account in deciding that she lacked the maturity to weigh her treatment options.

Judge Leblanc also said that he wants to have a guardian who is not related to the girl appointed to make treatment decisions on her behalf.

Adolescence is defined differently from province to province. In Newfoundland, children under 16 are considered not competent in law to make treatment decisions. Adults over the age of 19 are assumed to be competent even if a decision appears to go against their best interests.

EVALUATING THE AUTHOR'S ARGUMENTS:

This viewpoint was written by Kirk Makin about a case of severe self-injury in Newfoundland, Canada. In this Canadian province, individuals who are age sixteen and older are generally considered competent to make their own treatment decisions—including the right to refuse treatment. However, as the author explains, a judge ruled that it is sometimes necessary to take away this right if it is in an individual's best interests. What are the laws on the right to refuse treatment in your area? In your opinion, are these laws helpful or harmful to self-injurers? Explain.

Facts About Self-Injury

Editor's note: These facts can be used in reports to add credibility when making important points or claims.

The Frequency of Self-Injury

According to S.A.F.E. Alternatives (Self Abuse Finally Ends):

- One percent of the US population—2 to 3 million people—engage in some form of self-abusive behavior.
- In the United States, one out of every two hundred girls between the ages of thirteen and nineteen cut themselves regularly.
- Girls who cut make up 70 percent of teen girls who self-injure.

According to the Cornell Research Program on Self-Injurious Behavior:

- Thirteen to 24 percent of US and Canadian high school students self-injure.
- About 10 percent of British youth aged eleven to twenty-five self-injure.
- Seventeen percent of university students report having engaged in self-injury, with 11 percent indicating repeat self-injury.
- Sixty percent of self-injurers report that they do not wish to commit suicide.
- People with a history of self-injury are over nine times more likely to report suicide attempts.

According to University of South Florida researcher Moya L. Alfonso, 46 percent of surveyed youths report knowing someone who has harmed himself or herself.

Who Engages in Self-Injury?

According to the Cornell Research Program on Self-Injurious Behavior:

- Self-injury can start as early as age 7.

- Self-injury most often begins between the ages of 12 and 15.
- Thirty to 40 percent of college-aged self-injurers report that they started self-harming at age 17 or older.

According to University of South Florida researcher Moya L. Alfonso:
- Thirty-two percent of females and 25 percent of males have self-injured at least once.
- Thirty-two percent of people with eating disorders also self-injure.
- Sixty-six percent of those who have tried self-injury report that they know a friend who has also tried self-injury.
- Twenty percent of surveyed teen students who self-injure had previously been cyberbullied.
- Thirteen percent of surveyed teen students who self-injure had been physically hurt by a boyfriend or girlfriend within the previous twelve months.
- Seventy-eight percent of surveyed respondents who have attempted suicide had previously self-injured.
- Thirty-five percent of surveyed self-injuring youth have also made a suicide plan.

According to Parenting.org:
- Seventy-nine percent of self-injury callers to the Boys Town National Hotline are under age 18.
- Eighty-five percent of self-injury callers to the Boys Town National Hotline are female.
- Females who are 18 and under make up 67 percent of all self-injury callers to the Boys Town National Hotline.
- Nine percent of self-injury callers to the Boys Town National Hotline are between the ages of 19 and 23.

Reasons Young People Give for Self-Injury
- To stop feeling disconnected and numb
- To express pain and intense emotions
- To release tension or vent anger
- To calm and soothe oneself
- To gain a feeling of control when other aspects of life seem out of one's control

- To punish oneself
- To cry for help when it is too difficult to talk to someone
- Low self-esteem
- Mental health problems such as depression, anxiety, obsessive-compulsive disorder, or borderline personality disorder
- Peer pressure and curiosity

Organizations to Contact

The editors have compiled the following list of organizations concerned with the issues debated in this book. The descriptions are derived from materials provided by the organizations. All have publications or information available for interested readers. The list was compiled on the date of publication of the present volume; the information provided here may change. Be aware that many organizations take several weeks or longer to respond to inquiries, so allow as much time as possible for the receipt of requested materials.

Adolescent Self Injury Foundation (ASIF)
PO Box 962, South Haven, MI 49090
e-mail: adolescentselfinjuryfoundation@gmail.com
website: www.adolescentselfinjuryfoundation.com

The mission of the ASIF is to raise public awareness about adolescent self-injury. By providing educational resources, research, prevention techniques, and forums, the ASIF aims to enhance understanding about issues pertaining to self-harming teens and their families in the journey toward recovery and wellness. The home page features links to several fact sheets and reports, including "Understanding Adolescent Self-Injury," "The Do's and Don'ts for Parents," and "How Can I Help My Friend?"

American Psychiatric Association (APA)
1000 Wilson Blvd., Ste. 1825
Arlington, VA 22209-3901
(703) 907-7300
e-mail: apa@psych.org
website: www.psych.org

Founded in 1844, the APA is a professional organization dedicated to the nature, treatment, and prevention of mental disorders. The APA helps create mental health policies, distributes information about psychiatry, and promotes psychiatric research and education. It publishes the *American Journal of Psychiatry*, the newspaper *Psychiatric News*, and the quarterly journal *FOCUS*. The APA website also offers a searchable archive on a number of topics, including depression, anxiety disorders, and suicide.

American Psychological Association (APA)
750 First St. NE
Washington, DC 20002-4242
(800) 374-2421
(202) 336-5500
website: www.apa.org

The APA (not affiliated with the American Psychiatric Association although it uses the same acronym) is the largest professional organization of psychologists in the United States. Its mission is to foster the application of psychological knowledge to benefit society and improve people's lives. It produces numerous publications, including *American Psychologist*, *Psychological Review*, and the *Journal of Family Psychology*. The APA home page features a database with links to information on emotional health, teen mental health, anger, psychotherapy, and other topics.

Canadian Mental Health Association (CMHA)
595 Montreal Rd., Ste. 303
Ottawa, ON K1K 4L2 Canada
(613) 745-5522
website: www.cmha.ca

Founded in 1918, the CMHA is a voluntary organization that assists people suffering from mental illness in finding the help they need to cope with crises, regain confidence, and return to their communities, families, and jobs. The website includes an archive of links to dozens of articles on mental illness, including "Violence Towards People with Mental Health Problems," "Stigma and Mental Illness," and "Mental Health Promotion: A Framework for Action."

Depression and Bipolar Support Alliance
730 N. Franklin St., Ste. 501
Chicago, IL 60654-7225
(800) 826-3632
fax: (312) 642-7243
website: www.dbsalliance.org

The alliance provides support and advocacy for patients with depression and bipolar disorder. It asserts that these mood disorders are biochemical in nature and that no stigma should be placed on the people who suffer from them. The website features links to dozens of educational reports and brochures, including "Mood Disorders and Different Kinds of Depression," "Men and Depression," and "Is It Just a Mood . . . or Something Else? Mood Disorders for Young People."

Mental Health America
2000 N. Beauregard St., 6th Fl.
Alexandria, VA 22311
(703) 684-7722
(800) 969-6642
fax: (703) 684-5968
e-mail: info@mentalhealthamerica.net
website: www.nmha.org

Formerly known as the National Mental Health Association, Mental Health America strives to promote mental health and prevent mental disorders through advocacy, education, research, and service. The organization publishes fact sheets, position statements, and pamphlets on mental health policy. Its website offers links to information on self-injury, borderline personality disorder, depression in teens, and other mental health topics.

National Institute of Mental Health (NIMH)
6001 Executive Blvd.
Bethesda, MD 20892
(866) 615-6464
fax: (301) 443-4279
e-mail: nimhinfo@nih.gov
website: www.nimh.nih.gov

The NIMH is a government agency that seeks to improve the treatment and prevention of mental illness through research in neuroscience, behavioral science, and genetics. It publishes a variety of fact sheets and booklets on several mental illnesses. Its "Health Topics" archive includes a link to a page on Child and Adolescent Mental Health, which features the publications "Depression in Children and Adolescents" and "The Teen Brain: Still Under Construction."

National Self Harm Network (NSHN)

PO Box 7264
Nottingham NG1 6WJ United Kingdom
e-mail: support@nshn.co.uk
website: www.nshn.co.uk

The NSHN has been a United Kingdom–based survivor-led organization since 1994. A committed campaigner for the rights of people who self-injure, its priority is to support self-harmers, survivors, and the family and friends of self-harmers. Its publications include the poetry book *Silent Voices* and *The 'Hurt Yourself Less' Workbook*. The NSHN website offers links to fact sheets and brochures such as "What Is Self Harm?" and "Advice for Young People."

S.A.F.E. Alternatives

(800) 366-8288
fax: (888) 296-7988
e-mail: info@selfinjury.com
website: www.selfinjury.com

S.A.F.E. Alternatives, or Self Abuse Finally Ends, is a nationally recognized treatment approach, professional network, and educational resource base committed to helping self-harmers find a way out of self-injurious behavior. Its website features fact sheets, intervention tips, referrals to therapists, and multiple links to articles, interviews, and news video clips about self-injury.

Self-Injury and Related Isssues (SIARI)

website: www.palace.net/~llama/psych/injury.html

One of the largest self-injury resources on the web, SIARI aims to raise awareness about self-injury and to offer hope and support to self-injurers, their loved ones, and those who work alongside people who hurt themselves. Dozens of resources are available at this site, including fact sheets, articles, links to online communities and forums, and information pages such as "Frequently Asked Questions About Self-Injury," "Guide for Family and Friends," and "Deciding to Stop Self-Injuring."

For Further Reading

Books

Adler, Patricia A., and Peter Adler. *The Tender Cut: Inside the Hidden World of Self-Injury*. New York: New York University Press, 2011. Two sociology professors investigate the practice of self-injury from its early days, when few knew about the behavior, to the present day, in which subcultures of self-harmers can connect through the Internet. Their research draws on interviews with 150 self-injurers from all over the world.

Bowman, Susan, and Kaye Randall. *See My Pain! Creative Strategies and Activities for Helping Young People Who Self-Injure*. Chapin, SC: Youthlight, 2006. Explores the underlying causes of self-injury in children and teens and provides strategies and activities to help young people who deliberately harm themselves.

Leatham, Virginia. *Bloodletting: A True Story of Secrets, Self-Harm, and Survival*. London: Allison and Busby, 2006. A memoir of a young woman who struggled with cutting, eating disorders, substance abuse, and bipolar disorder, and the therapy that enabled her to face her problems.

Phillips, Alysa. *Stranger in My Skin*. Minneapolis: Word Warriors, 2006. The autobiography of a young girl growing up in a conventional Utah town who copes with physical, sexual, and emotional abuse by injuring herself.

Plante, Lori G. *Bleeding to Ease the Pain: Cutting, Self-Injury, and the Adolescent Search for Self*. Reissue. Lanham, MD: Rowman and Littlefield, 2010. The author maintains that self-inflicted wounds not only help numb the injurer and vent emotional pain, but can also be a dramatic way of communicating, controlling, and asking for help from others.

Rainfield, Cheryl. *Scars*. Lodi, NJ: WestSide, 2011. In this novel for young adults, a fifteen-year-old girl who is a survivor of sexual abuse cuts herself to cope with the pain. She finds emotional support through a friend, a teacher, a mentor, and a therapist. The book includes a resource section for youths seeking information on abuse, self-injury, dissociation, and related issues.

Shapiro, Lawrence. *Stopping the Pain: A Workbook for Teens Who Cut and Self-Injure*. Oakland, CA: Instant Help, 2008. Written by a child psychologist, this workbook helps youths who self-injure explore the reasons behind the need to hurt themselves and offers effective alternatives to self-harm.

Strong, Marilee. *A Bright Red Scream: Self-Mutilation and the Language of Pain*. New York: Penguin, 1999. A classic study on self-injury that explores the reasons that lead people to harm themselves as well as programs and treatments available to cutters. Includes interviews with over fifty self-injurers.

Sutton, Jan. *Healing the Hurt Within: Understand Self-Injury and Self-Harm, and Heal the Emotional Wounds*. 3rd ed. Oxford: How To Books, 2008. The author clarifies many of the myths and misconceptions surrounding self-injury, helping to reduce the stigma attached to this behavior.

Periodicals and Internet Sources

Bennett, Jessica. "Why She Cuts," *Newsweek*, December 29, 2008.

Bernhard, Blythe. "New Program Helps Those Who Self-Injure," *St. Louis (MO) Post-Dispatch*, September 3, 2009.

Brody, Jane E. "The Growing Wave of Teenage Self-Injury," *New York Times*, May 6, 2008.

Churchill, Theresa. "Self-Injury—A Call for Help, Expert Says," *Decatur (IL) Herald & Review*, March 25, 2010.

Corrigan, Don. "Self Injury, a Topic Not Often Talked About, May Affect 3 Million People," *Webster-Kirkwood Times* (Webster Groves, MO), April 15, 2011.

Crosby, Johanna. "A Journey from Self-Abuse to Self-Love," *Cape Cod (MA) Times*, May 29, 2008.

Hunter, Paul. "Chasing Down Demons: These Teens Run for a Better Life, Each Step Taking Them Further from the Clutches of Depression and Potential Self-Harm," *Toronto (ON) Star*, December 3, 2011.

Ingall, Marjorie. "Cutting Close," *Tablet Magazine*, May 17, 2011.

Jones, Lynn K. "Bleeding to Stop the Hurt: The Rise of Self-Injury," *Social Work Today*, May 2009.

Kowalski, Kathiann M. "The Unkindest Cut," *Current Health 2, a Weekly Reader Publication*, January 2008.

Larson, Nancy Fowler. "Self-Injury: Blood Flow Provides Escape for Bottled Up Feelings," *St. Louis (MO) Beacon*, June 7, 2010.

Moninger, Jeaneatte. "Cutting: Why Teens Hurt Themselves," *Family Circle*, July 2011.

Pedersen, Traci. "Ultrasound Technology Helpful in Treating Self-Harm Patients," Psych Central, September 9, 2010. http://psych central.com/news/2010/09/09/ultrasound-technology-helpful-in -treating-self-harm-patients/17894.html.

Picard, Andre. "One in Six Teens Inflict Self-Harm," *Toronto (ON) Globe and Mail*, January 29, 2008.

Prutsman, Tara. "My Shameful Secret," *Cosmopolitan*, February 2008.

Roan, Shari. "Self-Injury on the Rise Among Young People," *Los Angeles Times*, December 8, 2008.

Smith, Melinda, and Jeanne Segal. "Cutting and Self-Harm," Helpguide.org, June 2012. www.helpguide.org/mental/self_injury .htm.

Szabo, Liz. "Teens Share Internet Injury Videos," *USA Today*, February 21, 2011.

Thompson, Isha. "New Pageant Winner to Use Her Title to Speak Out," *Alberta Sweetgrass*, June 2010.

Townsend, Mark. "Special Report: 'The Walls Were Spattered with Blood Where She Banged Her Head,'" *Observer* (London), February 12, 2012.

Websites

Cornell Research Program on Self-Injurious Behavior in Adolescents and Young Adults (www.crpsib.com). This website provides fact sheets, links to articles, and numerous other resources for all seeking to better understand, detect, treat, and prevent self-injurious behavior in young people.

Psyke.org: Self-Injury Information and Support (www.psyke.org). This is a support website that includes fact sheets, coping suggestions, personal stories, and poetry about self-injury. An online message and discussion forum for self-injurers is also available.

Self-Harm: Recovery, Advice, and Support, TheSite.org (www .thesite.org/healthandwellbeing/mentalhealth/selfharm). Owned by the London-based charity YouthNet, TheSite.org is an online guide to life for sixteen- to twenty-five-year-olds. It provides nonjudgmental support and information on a wide variety of topics. The self-harm page on this website includes links to information about dealing with the urge to self-injure, low self-esteem, counseling, steps to recovery, and other topics; personal narratives and discussion boards are available as well.

Self-Injury and Related Issues (SIARI) (www.palace.net/~llama /psych/injury.html). This website offers information on self-injury and associated diagnoses such as mood disorders, borderline personality disorders, and eating disorders. It includes links to essays about causes, effects, and therapies for self-injury; coping strategies and suggestions for friends and family of self-harmers; and an interactive message board.

Index

Picture Credits

© AP Images/Scott Applewhite, 18

© Michael Ayre/Alamy, 53

© Design Pics Inc./Alamy, 13

© Gale/Cengage Learning, 15, 19, 23, 34, 41, 65, 67, 82, 90, 93, 105

© Justin Green/Alamy, 94

© Ian Hooten/Photo Researchers, Inc., 28

© itanistock/Alamy, 44

© Tim James/the Gray Gallery/Alamy, 48

© Janine Wiedel Photolibrary/Alamy, 11

© Steve Liss/Time Life Pictures/Getty Images, 84

© 1exposure/Alamy, 33

© Mark Phillips/Alamy, 81

© Tetra Images/Alamy, 89

© 20th Century Fox/the Kobal Collection at Art Resource, NY, 58